THE TABERNACLE OF GOD IN THE WILDERNESS OF SINAI

A packet of twenty-four slides containing most of the pictures found in this book is also available. These slides are in full color and clearly show the major details of the material and construction of the tabernacle and its sacrificial rites. (11067   ISBN 0-310-36218-0 $19.95)

THE TABERNACLE OF GOD IN THE WILDERNESS OF SINAI

Paul F. Kiene

Translated by
JOHN S. CRANDALL

ZONDERVAN PUBLISHING HOUSE OF THE ZONDERVAN CORPORATION
GRAND RAPIDS, MICHIGAN 49506

Das Heiligtum Gottes in der Wüste Sinai

ISBN 3-87739-283-0

THE TABERNACLE OF GOD IN THE WILDERNESS OF SINAI

Grand Rapids, Michigan

Library of Congress Cataloging in Publication Data

Kiene, Paul F
The tabernacle of God in the wilderness of Sinai.
Translation of *Das Heiligtum Gottes in der Wüste Sinai.*
1. Tabernacle. I. Title.
BM654.K4813 296.4 77-12986
ISBN 0-310-36200-8

Printed in the United States of America

The picture of the high priest on page 165 is courtesy of Aquarell von Arthur Rossel-Blaser.

Scripture passages are from the King James Version unless marked otherwise.

The Tabernacle of God

– the place where He manifested His glory in judgment and grace, the dwelling place of the Almighty among His people on the basis of the expiatory offering.

"And let them make me a sanctuary; that I may dwell among them" (Exodus 25:8).

Contents

Illustrations / 8

The Makeup of the Tabernacle / 9

The Names of the Tabernacle / 11

Preface / 12

1. *Introduction* / 15
   The Tent of Meeting
   The Spiritual Meaning of the Dwelling Place of God
   Divine Instructions for Building the Tabernacle
   The Tabernacle in the Wilderness of Sinai
   The Heave Offering for God
   The Fourteen Components of the Heave Offering

2. *The Outer Court* / 31
   The Outer Court of the Tabernacle
   The Exterior of the Outer Court
   The Hangings of the Outer Court
   Within the Outer Court
   The Brazen Altar With Its Grating
   The Brazen Laver With Its Stand

3. *The Tabernacle Structure* / 67
The Exterior of the Tabernacle
The Covering of Badgers' Skins
The Covering of Rams' Skins
The Covering of Goats' Hair
The Four-colored Cherubim Covering
The Entrance to the Tabernacle
The Five Pillars of the Entrance to the Tabernacle
The Golden Walls of the Tabernacle
The Boards of the Dwelling Place
The Poles

4. *The Holy Place* / 99
The Interior of the Tabernacle
The Table of Shewbread
The Shewbread
The Pure Candlestick
The Light of the Candlestick
The Holy Vessels of the High Priest
The Golden Altar of Incense

5. *The Holy of Holies* / 133
The Veil
The Four Pillars of the Veil
The Ark of the Covenant
The Mercy Seat With the Cherubim
The Contents of the Ark of the Covenant
The Ark of the Covenant in the Holy of Holies
The Holy Garments of the High Priest
The Completed Work

ILLUSTRATIONS

The Courtyard With the Tabernacle / 19
At the Gate of the Outer Courtyard / 33
The Hanging of the Gate / 34
A Single Pillar of the Courtyard / 41
The Morning Offering / 48
A Sacrificial Scene at Noon / 53
The Presentation and Slaughtering of the Animals / 56
The Brazen Altar and Its Grating / 59
The Brazen Laver With Priests / 63
The Laver and Its Stand / 65
The Tabernacle With Its Four Coverings / 69
The Badger-Skin and Ram-Skin Coverings / 73
The Goats'-Hair and the Cherubim Coverings / 74
The Ten-Part Cherubim Covering / 80
The Cherubim Covering With the Golden Clasps / 81
The Entrance to the Tabernacle With the Curtain / 86
The Five Pillars to the Entrance of the Tabernacle / 91
The Golden Walls of the Tabernacle / 92
The Golden Boards of the Dwelling Place of God / 95
The West Wall With Its Poles / 97
The Inside of the Tabernacle With the
Three Articles of Furniture / 102
The Golden Table of Shewbread / 107
The Golden Candlestick / 115
The Golden Altar of Incense and the
Golden Vessels of the Tabernacle / 120
The Four-colored Veil / 125
The Four Pillars of the Veil / 138
The Ark of the Covenant With the Cherubim / 141
The Golden Mercy Seat / 148
The Open Ark of the Covenant With Its Contents / 151
The Ark of the Covenant in the Holy of Holies / 158
The High Priest in Holy Garments / 165
The Tabernacle With the Cloudy Pillar / 174

THE MAKEUP OF THE TABERNACLE

The Freewill Heave Offering; the Material of the Tabernacle

Fourteen components: gold, silver, brass, blue, purple, scarlet, byssus, goats' hair, rams' skins dyed red, badgers' skins, acacia wood, oil, spices, precious stones. Exodus 25:1–9; 30:13–15; 35:5–29; 36:2–7; cf. Genesis 15:13–14.

The Outer Court

The entrance gate with the wide, four-colored curtain. The pillars of acacia wood with the copper bases and silver capitals. The hangings of white byssus on the silver fillets. The pins of brass. Exodus 27:1–19; 38:17–20; Numbers 4:26,32.

The brazen altar with the brass grating and the staves. The brazen laver with its stand. The instruments and vessels of brass that belonged to these. Exodus 27:1–8; 30:17–21; 38:1–8; Numbers 4:13–14.

The Exterior of the Tabernacle

The five golden pillars with the brass bases and golden capitals. The entrance curtain with the four colors. The two coverings of skins and the two woven coverings of the tent. The three walls of the tabernacle — made of wood overlaid with gold. The five golden poles for each wall. Exodus 26:1–3,36–37; 36:8–34,37–38; Numbers 4:25,31.

The Holy Place

The golden table with the twelve loaves of shewbread and the drink offering. The golden candlestick with its six branches and seven lamps. The golden altar of incense with the four horns and the staves. The golden instruments and vessels that belonged to these. Exodus 25: 23–40; 30:1–10; 37:10–28; 39:36–37; Leviticus 24:1–9; Numbers 4:7,11–12.

The Holy of Holies

The four golden pillars with the silver bases. The four-colored veil with the cherubim. The golden ark of the covenant with the staves. The golden mercy seat with the cherubim. Exodus 25:10–22; 26:31–33; 36:35–36; 37:1–9; Numbers 4:5,31; Hebrews 9:5.

The high priest in the holy garments. Exodus 28:1–40; 39:1–31; Leviticus 8:1–9.

The completed work. Exodus 39:32–43; 40:17–38; Numbers 9:15–16.

THE NAMES OF THE TABERNACLE

The tent of meeting	Exodus 27:21
The tabernacle of Jehovah	Leviticus 17:4
The tabernacle of testimony	Numbers 1:50
The tent of the testimony	Numbers 9:15
The sanctuary of Jehovah	Numbers 19:20
The house of God	Judges 18:31
The house of Jehovah	1 Samuel 1:7
The temple of Jehovah	1 Samuel 1:9
The tabernacle of the testimony	Acts 7:44
A sanctuary of this world	Hebrews 9:1

Because they best translate the German, these designations are taken from the American Standard Version.

PREFACE

This book is addressed to all those whom God greets with the words "Grace be with all them that love our Lord Jesus Christ in sincerity" (Ephesians 6:24).

Everyone who loves Him will be moved in his innermost being when the Scriptures are opened and he recognizes in them the One of whom the prophets spoke in former times. The Spirit of Christ who was in them used many pictures to portray His suffering and glory (1 Peter 1:11).

May His wisdom lead us as we elucidate the types of Christ in the tabernacle. This holy, unique construction speaks of Him in all of its details. Throughout we see the magnificent greatness of His wonderful person with wonder and amazement. At the same time we also see how His perfect work of salvation is prophetically represented in the sacrificial acts. Thus, the Word of God by the mouth of the prophet is fulfilled: "My counsel shall stand, and I will do all my pleasure" (Isaiah 46:10).

May the Holy Spirit illuminate our understanding so that we may comprehend the wonderful details of the tabernacle. May the unparalleled humiliation of Christ, as well as His wonderful majesty, awaken worshipful homage in our hearts. His name be eternally honored!

THE TABERNACLE OF GOD IN THE WILDERNESS OF SINAI

The blood of the Substitute paves the way to God for the sinner and opens the entrance to the Holy of Holies for the worshiper.

"Jehovah, I love the habitation of thy house, and the place where thy glory dwelleth" (Psalm 26:8 ASV).

"And in his temple doth every one speak of his glory" (Psalm 29:9).

"How amiable are thy tabernacles, O LORD of hosts! My soul longeth, yea, even fainteth for the courts of the LORD; my heart and my flesh cry out for the living God" (Psalm 84:1–2).

1. *Introduction*

THE TENT OF MEETING

The tabernacle of God in the wilderness of Sinai is the first habitation that the living God ever caused to be built for Him. During the forty days and nights Moses spent on the holy mountain, he received not only the tables with the commandments of God, but also the divine instructions for this unique construction.

The people who had been redeemed out of Egypt were allowed to bring a freewill heave offering, according to the instruction of God, to make possible the building of the tabernacle: acacia wood, animal skins, and spun yarn, as well as metals and precious stones.

Fourteen different kinds of materials were used by artisans for the production of the tabernacle. In the course of one year, the tabernacle was erected at the base of Sinai. Almighty God attested His pleasure with this habitation by His presence in the bright cloudy pillar: "Then the cloud covered the tent of meeting, and the glory of Jehovah filled the tabernacle" (Exodus 40:34 ASV).

For about 500 years services were performed in this tabernacle by the priests who were from the family of Aaron. These services consisted of the presentation of the many offerings and worshipful homage through the burning of holy incense before the Lord. This tent was also the place God manifested Himself, where He proclaimed His thoughts and council through Moses: "I will commune with thee from above the mercy-seat, from between the two cherubim which are upon the ark of the testimony" (Exodus 25:22).

In the Bible the habitation of God is called the "tent of meeting" 144 times, a highly significant designation. God's desire for fellowship with man was to find its fulfillment there. Through the Anointed One of God, Jesus Christ, it was and will be a reality.

THE SPIRITUAL MEANING OF THE DWELLING PLACE OF GOD

"For whatsoever things were written aforetime were written for our learning" (Romans 15:4).

"Moses . . . wrote of me" (John 5:46; cf. v. 39).

"And beginning from Moses and from all the prophets, he interpreted to them in all the scriptures the things concerning himself" (Luke 24:27 ASV; cf. v. 44).

These are the words of the Holy Spirit in the New Testament concerning the declarations about, and prophetic references to, Christ in the writings of Old Testament witnesses.

The Book of Hebrews very clearly explains the symbolic meaning of the Mosaic order of worship in the tabernacle as dealing with the "shadow of the heavenly things . . . with a holy place made with hands, like in pattern to the true" — a copy and shadow of heavenly things according to the divine instruction given to Moses: "See . . . that thou make all things according to the pattern that was showed thee in the mount" (Hebrews 8:5; 9:23–24 ASV).

These expressions of the Word of God reveal the symbolic significance of the tent of meeting, thus opening our eyes to the fact that this tabernacle speaks of God something yet greater. God graphically reveals here something of what Paul in the Book of Ephesians calls "the mystery of Christ" (Ephesians 3:3,4). In a wonderful way He shows something of His eternal purpose that He accomplished in Christ Jesus: the glorification of Christ and His assembly, of the church of all those who were sealed by the Holy Spirit.

Redeemed and spiritually minded people will be inwardly arrested by the account concerning the tabernacle. The more they grasp of its wonderful meaning, the more they yearn to penetrate deeper and deeper into the secrets of the plans of God.

DIVINE INSTRUCTION FOR BUILDING THE TABERNACLE

The Holy Spirit has spoken in Genesis 1:1 of the miraculous work of God's creation. For that purpose He used only a few simple words: "In the beginning God created the heavens and the earth." Men would have used innumerable volumes to write about their splendid work. Not so the Creator of the universe. His incomparable work speaks for itself and gives testimony to His glory.

But when God spoke concerning His dwelling place on earth and of that which is connected with it, He chose, to our amazement, a much more detailed description. The construction and the arrangement of His dwelling in the wilderness, as well as all things pertaining to the priesthood, the sacrifices, and the worship service, are extremely significant and important to Him. God uses, therefore, fifty chapters in the Pentateuch and Hebrews

A tent such as this was the first habitation of God on earth. In the forty days and nights that Moses spent on Mt. Sinai, he received the tables of the law and, at the same time, the instructions of God for the construction of the tabernacle. The materials came from Israel's freewill gifts.

for its description. Creation forms, as it were, only the backdrop for the tabernacle of God.

In his song in Exodus 15, Moses as prophet had already sung prophetically to the glory of God with the people of Israel: "The LORD is my strength and my song, and he is become my salvation: He is my God, and I will prepare him a habitation" (v. 2).

According to divine decree, this song of praise was realized through the construction of the habitation of Jehovah. Here the heavenly things were made visible on earth.

For believers, who are called "partakers of a heavenly calling," all this has special meaning. To them, the tabernacle of God is of perfect beauty and has spiritually attractive power.

THE TABERNACLE IN THE WILDERNESS OF SINAI

Here we see the tabernacle within the outer court, which consisted of sixty pillars, twenty each on the north and south sides and ten each on the east and west sides. They were all bound together by silver rods. From these rods hung a white byssus hanging, whose total length was 280 cubits. On the east side was the single entrance, a curtain of four colors. In the middle of the outer court stood the brazen altar for burnt offerings on a mound of sand. To the north there were several slaughtering benches. The brazen laver stood between the brazen altar and the tabernacle. From the tabernacle itself one saw only the five pillars of the entrance, which supported the curtain of the gate. The remaining part of the tabernacle was covered with the outermost veil of badger skins.

THE HEAVE OFFERING FOR GOD

As the living God was about to lead His people out of Egypt, He commanded Israel before their departure from the house of bondage to ask for gold and silver articles and clothes from their heathen neighbors. Because of the horrible plagues, the Egyptians were gripped with terror. They were glad to be rid of these people at last and were therefore ready to give those who departed what they desired. In this manner the children of Israel "despoiled" the Egyptians (Exodus 3:22; 11:2; 12:36).

Was that not a fitting compensation for the labor they had rendered during their many years of slavery? The promise had been given 430 years previously to Abraham that his seed would be freed from slavery and depart with great substance (Genesis 15:14).

In this way the people of God possessed enough to dedicate a heave offering to the "Holy One of Israel" for the construction of a tabernacle or temple. For that purpose, of course, a great quantity of material was necessary. This kind of offering was called a "heave offering" because such gifts were lifted up toward heaven by the donor and in this way were dedicated to God. God tested the hearts of the people who had been redeemed from servitude, requiring them through Moses to bring Him this offering. Not long before, they had offended the majesty of God with the casting of the golden calf. On that occasion they had shamefully squandered a part of their gold. The divine response was a terrible judgment. After that, they had to hear the bitter words from the mouth of the Lord: "Now put off thy ornaments from thee, that I may know what to do unto thee. And the children of Israel stripped themselves of their ornaments by the mount Horeb" (Exodus 33:5–6). Was this not a clear sign of the emotion of their hearts? "They mourned: and no man did put on him his ornaments" (v. 4).

Only from a people so humbled could a holy God accept freewill gifts.

"And all the congregation of the children of Israel departed from the presence of Moses. And they came, every one whose heart stirred him up, and every one whom his spirit made willing, and brought Jehovah's offering, for the work of the tent of meeting, and for all the service thereof, and for the holy garments. And they came, both men and women, as many as were willing-hearted, and brought brooches, and ear-rings and signet-rings, and armlets, all jewels of gold; even every man that offered an offering of gold unto Jehovah. And every man, with whom was found blue, and purple, and scarlet, and fine linen, and goats' hair and rams' skins dyed red, and sealskins, brought them. Every one that did offer an offering of silver and brass brought Jehovah's offering; and every man, with whom was found acacia wood for any work of the service, brought it. And all the women that were wise-hearted did spin with their hands, and brought that which they had spun, the blue, and the purple, the scarlet, and the fine linen. And all the women whose heart stirred them up in wisdom spun the goats' hair. And the rulers brought the onyx stones, and the stones to be set, for the ephod, and for the breastplate; and the spice, and the oil; for the light, and for the anointing oil, and for the sweet incense. The children of Israel brought a freewill-offering unto Jehovah; every man and woman, whose heart made them willing to bring for all the work, which Jehovah had commanded to be made by Moses" (Exodus 35:20–29 ASV).

The effect was astounding. To glorify the Lord the Israelites gave with happy hearts for this work. Each one whose heart moved him, each who was of willing spirit, contributed to it with his offering.

One might say that it was "first love" that filled their hearts and moved them to action (Exodus 35:4–36:7).

In this they are an example that spurs us to emulation. Jesus Christ, who has freed us from eternal death and has saved us from the power of Satan, is worthy of such voluntary support for His work from us also today. Thus, we read that there were at one time believers in Macedonia of whom it could be said: "First they gave their own selves to the Lord" and "according to their power . . . and beyond their power, they gave of their own accord" (2 Corinthians 8:1-5).

"The people bring much more than enough. . . ." This joyful report was given to Moses by the colaborers. Thereupon the people were "restrained from bringing" (Exodus 36:5,6).

Is it also our wish and desire to give all for the house of God? Or does the Lord's accusation apply to us: "Will a man rob God? Yet ye have robbed me. But ye say, Wherein have we robbed thee? In tithes and offerings.[1] Ye are cursed with a curse: for ye have robbed me, even this whole nation. . . . Prove me now herewith, saith the Lord of hosts, if I will not open you the windows of heaven, and pour you out a blessing, that there shall not be room enough to receive it" (Malachi 3:8-10).

David, the man after God's own heart, experienced this blessing. He demonstrated genuine, living interest in the house of God and prepared the building material for the construction of the temple in Jerusalem. He was also a stimulus for the people of that time to give and to work. The result was great joy because of the willingness of the contributors. Out of an overflowing heart, David praised his God for it (1 Chronicles 28:11–29:22).

Through the heave offering in the wilderness, the construction material for the tabernacle was gathered. Now it was time to fashion these materials. This required divine wisdom, which is mentioned seven times in this connection. In particular, the Spirit of God filled two gifted men with this wisdom: Bezaleel and Aholiab. He made them skilled craftsmen, who at the same time also were the instructors for their co-workers. They instructed each one whose heart God had made willing, to aid in the construction of His house. What an impressive picture! Multitudes of people, compelled by their hearts to help, wise-hearted men and women (Exodus 35:21–29; 36:2).

[1]The German edition reads: "In tithes and *heave offerings.*"

There were also at one time in Corinth volunteer co-laborers in the work of the Lord. They are mentioned by name as a sign of recognition and approval of their service of love: the house of Stephanas devoted itself to the ministry of the saints along with all others who toiled and labored (1 Corinthians 16:15–16). Then, as now, the saints built the house of God. They were the church of Jesus Christ and His temple. Are you also devoted to this Lord and His house?

Moses and his band of co-workers were able within the space of one year to erect the tabernacle according to the plan and thoughts of God. They experienced that most holy moment when the cloud of the glory of God filled the dwelling place. Thus, a holy place was made and dedicated where the Eternal One could have wonderful fellowship with His redeemed people (Exodus 40:34–38).

For the first time since the creation of the worlds there was now erected for God a dwelling place on this earth, built according to the heavenly example.

THE FOURTEEN COMPONENTS OF THE HEAVE OFFERING

Some Facts About the Offering

1. *Gold.* In the Bible, gold, especially pure gold, is considered the most valuable of all available metals. Gold is mentioned eighty times in connection with the heave offering; but pure, refined, genuine gold only twenty-one times. The weight of the wave offering in gold totaled 29 talents and 730 shekels, about 1.5 metric tons (1.65 tons) (Exodus 38:24).

2. *Silver.* The second most precious metal, silver, is

mentioned twenty-two times in connection with the construction of God's tabernacle. The total weight of the silver that was used is given as 100 talents and 1,775 shekels. That is approximately 4.4 metric tons (4.85 tons).

This silver was derived from the atonement money of the mustered military personel of Israel — money that God had required of each one personally. In Exodus 30:11–16; 38:25–28, one-half of a shekel, equal to ten gerahs, was required of each warrior. Every grown man who entered into God's service was called upon to give this atonement money. At the same time he received for this a "memorial" part in the tabernacle, because the silver was used there. Atonement money is mentioned fourteen times in the Bible.

3. *Brass.* The term *brass* actually means "bronze." The bronze of antiquity originated mostly from the island of Cyprus, hence the Latin name *cuprum.* This extremely fire-resistant metal was named thirty-five times in its use for the tabernacle. The weight of the brass that was dedicated to the Lord as a wave offering totaled seven talents and 2,400 shekels, which is about three metric tons (3.3 tons). This important metal, out of which many articles in the courtyard were made, is known for its exceptional strength. Its resistance to fire is very great; its melting point is 1,085°C (1,985° F) and is, therefore, higher than that of gold, which is 1,069°C (1,949°F).

4. *Blue.* For the description of this color, the Hebrew used the designation *kehelet,* meaning thereby a deep but bright violet. Such color tones are seen in the heavens of the East.

This fabric, made of twisted thread the color of the sky,

served for making the hangings of the gate and the covering of the tabernacle. It is mentioned thirty-six times.

5. *Purple.* This indicates a dark red yarn for artistic weaving and embroidery. The purple color was gained by the secretion of a gland of the purple snail *(Murex).* This material is named twenty-seven times.

6. *Scarlet.* Scarlet is the color of arterial blood; it is also known as crimson. The latter name comes from the Persian word *kermes,* meaning "worm." The kermes shield-louse, called "coccus ilicis" or "coccinos," fixes itself to the leaves of the holly plant. Their maggots were collected, then dried and pulverized, and this powder produced a red dye for the dying of the yarn. The rope that Rahab was told to tie in the window for her salvation (Joshua 2:18) was bright scarlet. Scarlet is named as a component of the heave offering twenty-seven times.

7. *Byssus.* Byssus is the seventh component of the heave offering. The Hebrew word is *shech.* Because of its color, it is called *bûs* in Aramaic, from which the Greek name *byssos* surely originated. Egyptologist Wilkinson found byssus in the tombs of pharaohs and counted the threads in order to ascertain the fineness of the weave. He found along a one-inch length (25.4 mm) 152 threads in the warp and 71 threads in the woof.[2] The finest cotton weave produced today with the best technical methods contains in comparison only 86 threads per inch.

This clearly shows the unheard-of fineness and costliness of the byssus linen, which is mentioned thirty-six times.

8. *Goats' hair.* Long-haired goats are numerous in the

[2]Urquart, *Die neueren Entdeckungen und die Bibel* (Stuttgart: Kielmann, 1903), p. 99.

Orient. They forage among the thorn bushes of the desert, and hair that is caught in the bushes can be collected by children.

The heave offering for making the tent coverings consisted of spun goats' hair. It is mentioned six times.

9. *Rams' skins.* The skins of rams were dyed red. They made up the second skin covering of the tabernacle and are also mentioned six times. In Genesis 22:13 the ram was the sacrificial animal that died as a substitute for Isaac. The ram was also the sacrifice that was brought at the dedication of the priests of God (Exodus 29:1–35).

10. *Badgers' skins.* The Hebrew word *tachash* is translated in different ways. As a component of the heave offering, it means "badger skin." In Ezekiel 16:10 we find the corresponding word translated as "sealskin" or "porpoise-skin" (see ASV). It may even be the skin of coneys (Psalm 104:18; Proverbs 30:26). Badgers' skins are mentioned ten times.

11. *Acacia wood.* The acacia is a species of mimosa, whose wood is darker and harder than oak and is very durable, being therefore avoided by the wood-eating insects. In the Greek translation of the Old Testament, the Septuagint, acacia wood is rendered very appropriately as "incorruptible wood."

12. *Oil.* What is meant here is pure oil from ripe olives (Leviticus 24:2). The olives were carefully crushed in a mortar. The first drops were of especially pure quality. They served as fuel for the seven lamps of the candelabra of pure gold.

13. *Spices.* The four best spices for the anointing oil were the following (Exodus 30:22–25):

Myrrh is the sap of the balsam bush. It either exudes of itself from the rind or it runs, like tears, out of a wound or cut in the stem. In Song of Solomon 4:14 it is considered one of the chief spices.

Cinnamon is the bark of a beautiful tree with shiny green leaves. The cinnamon tree, Latin *cinnamomum cassia,* is a species of laurel bush.

Sweet calamus is the pink-colored pith from the root of a reed plant, out of which perfume is produced.

Cassia comes from the dried flowers of the cinnamon tree. It was a component of a sweet-smelling ointment (Psalm 45:8).

The four sweet-smelling spices for the incense were the following (Exodus 30:34-38):

Stacte was a powder obtained from the middle of the hardened drops of the myrrh bush; it was a very rare substance and therefore most valuable.

Onycha was derived from the shell of a kind of clam that has a certain similarity to the purple snail. The best clams of this type are found in the deep part of the Red Sea.

Galbanum is a rubbery resin of the thickened milky juice from the roots of a species of ferula. This flowering plant grows about two meters (2.19 yards) high and thrives in Syria and Persia. The odor of its resin is pungent and is pleasing only when the resin is mixed with other spices.

Frankincense is the transparent or white resin from the bark of a bush or tree that carries the botanical name, *Boswellia carteri.* This resin was pulverized in mortars and served as a holy incense. It was also added to the meal offering (Leviticus 2:1).

Frankincense was placed on the shewbread and burned there, but it was never allowed to be used with the burnt offering (Leviticus 24:7; 5:11).

14. *The Precious Stones.* Twelve precious stones were selected for the breastplate of the high priest. They were arranged one row under another in four rows of threes. Their sequence, from left to right and from top to bottom, were:[3]

Sardis, brownish red; *topaz,* yellow to yellowish red; *emerald,* clear green.

Carbuncle, red garnet; *sapphire,* deep blue; *diamond,* sparkling white.

Amber, bright yellow; *agate,* delicate blue; *amethyst,* violet.

Beryl, green-yellow; *onyx,* bright yellow; *jasper,* pure and clear.

However, the listing in Hebrew is given from right to left.

The Components of the Heave Offering and Their Symbolic Meaning

All of these materials offered point to the glory of the Lord Jesus Christ and His work of redemption.

Here are the possibilities of their inner meaning:

Gold — the Holy, Just, and Perfect One; His majesty and glory.

Silver — the Reconciler, Savior, and Redeemer; the atonement for our sins.

Brass — the Tested, Suffering, and Judged One, who withstood the fury of God's wrath.

[3]For these colors see the American Standard Version.

Blue — the Son of God, in accordance with His heavenly being and origin.

Purple — the King of Kings and Lord of Lords, the Prince of the kings of the earth.

Scarlet — the Servant of God as the sacrificial Lamb; His suffering and His glory as the Messiah of Israel.

White Byssus — the Son of Man in His spotless purity and sinlessness.

Spun Goats' Hair — the faithful and true Witness, the Prophet of God in simplicity and poverty.

Red-dyed Rams' Skins — the Leader and Protector of His flock; symbol of His dedication and His submission even to death.

Badgers' Skins — the separated and lonely One, who guards the honor of God.

Acacia Wood — The Shoot from the stump of Jesse, the Branch out of the lineage of David.

Olive Oil —The Reflection of God as His Anointed, full of the Holy Spirit and power.

Sweet-smelling Spices — the fragrant Perfume for God, the Joy for the heart of the Father.

Selected Precious Stones — His selected ones, highly valued of God, because He bought them at great cost.

The Dimensions and Numbers

For the construction and the furnishing of the tabernacle God gave various dimensions and numbers. They were given by God as instructions for the construction of the whole. His wisdom comes to visible expression in them.

The symbolic value of numbers in the Bible is uncontested. The sober, intelligent evaluation and application of them can convincingly influence heart and mind. Often they yield spiritual insights and perceptions that serve to enrich and deepen the inner life of faith.

The unit of measure used for construction at that time was the old Hebrew cubit (52.52 cm or 20.7 inches).

The dry measure, called an ephah, had a capacity of 22 liters (23.2 quarts).

2. *The Outer Court*

THE OUTER COURT OF THE TABERNACLE

"Blessed is the man whom thou choosest, and causest to approach unto thee, that he may dwell in thy courts" (Psalm 65:4).

"My soul longeth, yea, even fainteth for the courts of the LORD: my heart and my flesh crieth out for the living God" (Psalm 84:2).

What, then, did the believer find in that oft-mentioned place, the court of the tabernacle?

He found the blessedness and satisfaction of goodness (Psalm 65;4); fulfillment of his yearning for the living God (Psalm 84:2); the best days of his life (Psalm 84:10); the revival of his faith: flourishing life (Psalm 92:12); and the bringing of offerings to God in worship (Psalm 96:8).

The eager desire to be there filled the heart of the God-fearing Israelite. The psalm-singers were deeply stirred when they thought of the outer court. The blessedness of the believers began here when they appeared before the face of God to bring their various offerings.

In the picture on page 33 we see a man attempting to enter through the curtained gate into the outer court with an animal sacrifice. Two porters (1 Chronicles 9:17–23) refuse him entry, prohibiting him from coming into

Porters guard the entrance to the outer court. They are refusing an Israelite entrance because he is trying to bring an unclean animal as an offering. He must exchange the donkey for a lamb.

God's presence with this animal. If this man had presented it in sacrifice, it would have meant certain death for him. He had not observed what God had said in Leviticus 11:3 about the animals that were appropriate as a sacrifice for God. Only animals that were both cud-chewing and split-hooved were clean and could be used as an offering. A donkey is neither the one nor the other.

How then could one who had become guilty obtain forgiveness? He was required to choose an offering from the lambs and sheep that were at his disposal.

This Israelite is an appropriate picture for all those who, following their own thinking, attempt to clear themselves with God. They believe they can obtain God's grace through their good works, as it is written: ". . . after the commandments and doctrines of men? Which things have indeed a shew of wisdom in will-worship" (Colossians 2:22–23). This widely held error is exposed by the Lord in Matthew 15:9 with the words: "But in vain they do worship me, teaching for doctrines the commandments of men."

With the utmost distinctness, the Word of God speaks of salvation in the following declaration: "For *by grace* are ye saved through faith . . . *not* of works, lest any man should boast" (Ephesians 2:8–9). "And if by grace, then is it no more of works: otherwise grace is no more grace" (Romans 11:6).

But perhaps this man had wanted to *redeem* the firstborn of his donkey in order to preserve its life. God required in Exodus 13:13 that all the firstborn of man and animal should belong to Him, and that it be brought to Him as a sacrifice. In this law God invoked the requirement that the firstborn of the donkey and of man had to be

redeemed through a lamb. This lamb was slain in place of the one to be redeemed. God put man on a par with the unclean donkey with this directive: Both had to be redeemed, or they would certainly die.

What a wonderful provision of God! We know the Lamb who acquired salvation from deserved judgment for us unclean ones once and for all. Let us continually praise and adore His holy name.

We learn here the truth of the divine utterance in Exodus 34:20 and Deuteronomy 16:16: "And none shall appear before me empty." Only with an acceptable sacrifice can man come near to the living God and enter into His holy presence. This is why the Lord Jesus spoke these most important, highly significant words: "No man cometh unto the Father, but by me" (John 14:6).

THE EXTERIOR OF THE OUTER COURT

The Gate With the Four-colored Curtain

The only door through which one could gain entrance to the outer court was located on the east side. Illuminated

by the morning sun, it presents and arresting sight to the eyes of the passerby. A gorgeous embroidery in four bright colors attracts his gaze. It is a wide entrance door—an invitation for everyone to enter into the holy place. Let us say right from the beginning that here for the first time we see a wonderful picture that points to the Savior.

The Dimensions of the Gate

Its width is of an inviting size: a full 20 cubits. The Lord Jesus Christ stands before us, so to speak, with outstretched arms and with encouraging, alluring words: "Come unto me, all ye that labour and are heavy laden, and I will give you rest" (Matthew 11:28). Here is symbolically presented what the people from Sychar discovered one day with happy hearts, testifying: "This is indeed the Christ, the Saviour of the world" (John 4:42). Twenty cubits is a width of 4 times 5 cubits; because we speak of the four corners of the world, four is thought to be the number of the world's width, five (a lowly number) the number of the man who is dependent upon God. This is to tell us that the good news of Jesus has world-wide

On the east side of the courtyard hung the colored curtain-gate. Its four colors were blue, purple, scarlet (or crimson), and white byssus. It was 20 cubits long and 5 cubits high. Easily seen from a distance, it was an invitation for all who desired to come near to God.

significance and applies to all men! The height of the gate totaled 5 cubits: by so much did the Lord Jesus humble Himself. He, the Creator of the worlds, became a dependent man!

The Four Colors of the Hanging

All the details of the tabernacle constitute a glorious, impressive, pictorial language of God. They point prophetically to the coming Savior and to the full and efficacious salvation that He was to bring. The New Testament gives us light and clarity to understand these portraits. In them we can perceive the message of the gospel with great joy.

The four colors may correspond to the four evangelists. Each color conforms to one of the conspicuously glorious characteristics of the Lord Jesus that the Holy Spirit desires to emphasize in these divine documents. To discover this moves the heart of the believer to a worshipful sense of wonder because of divine wisdom.

Now the individual colors: blue, purple, scarlet, and white byssus. Their significance merits careful investigation, for they appear in the three entrance hangings, as well as in the cherubim covering over the tabernacle. They are also found in the robe and belt of the high priest and in the belts of the priests' sons.

In addition, there also appears to be a connection between these four colors and the mysterious forms of the "four living creatures," whom we meet over thirty times in the Bible (in the prophet Ezekiel and in Revelation).

Blue. Blue may be said to represent the *Gospel of John*. This apostle described our Lord as the eternal Son of God who came from heaven. How often we hear Him say of Himself that He has "come out of heaven" (John 3:13,31;

6:32–33,58). We hear in His own words almost forty times that He was the One sent of the Father as the heavenly Messenger of divine love. He was the second man, the second Adam, and, coming from heaven, He bore the name "the man of heaven" (1 Corinthians 15:47–49). He came to tell us "of heavenly things" (John 3:12). Accordingly, one of the four living creatures in Revelation 4:7 appears "like a flying eagle" whose element is the wide, blue heaven.

Purple. This reminds us vividly of the glory of Jesus Christ, who is the King of Kings and the Messiah of Israel, just as the evangelist Matthew especially shows Him. The purple robe is one of the coronation robes of many kings. In antiquity purple was a sign of highest might. Thus, purple is thoroughly appropriate for the Lord Jesus to whom is due the highest glory and honor that He will one day receive on this earth. Only in the *Gospel of Matthew* do we find the question right at the beginning: "Where is he that is born King of the Jews?" Nine times in Matthew He receives the title of a king. In the Old Testament the Lord Jesus is so named fifty times. Likewise, the first living creature in Revelation 4 symbolically represents this honor: "And the first beast was like a lion," and in Revelation 5 the almighty Ruler is called "the lion of the tribe of Judah." He has the unique claim to the title to the throne of David and will victoriously possess it.

Scarlet. As mentioned in regard to the heave offering, the word *crimson* (used in some translations) is derived from the Persian word *kermes* and means "worm." The color tone is scarlet and reminds one of arterial blood.

The designation *worm* is certainly the strongest expression for helplessness: naked, defenseless, blind, and powerless! Thus Bildad characterized the lost sinner in Job 25:4–6: "How much less man, that is a worm? and the son of man, which is a worm?" With such the Son of God *made Himself one,* in order to bear as their substitute the wrath of God they deserved. The heart-gripping words of the Crucified One in Psalm 22:6 allow us to see something of His deepest degradation, distress, and shame, when He cried out; "But I am a worm, and no man . . . ." To the Lord Jesus Christ belongs adoring homage, for we are indebted to Him for this great salvation.

In the *Gospel of Mark* we can see Him as the One who said of Himself: "For even the Son of man came not to be ministered unto, but to minister, and to give his life a ransom for many" (Mark 10:45). The scarlet — the color of blood — should remind us of this suffering Servant of God wherever we see it in the component materials of the tabernacle.

Moreover, we can recognize the earthly and messianic glory of the Lord Jesus Christ in the scarlet-colored clothing (2 Samuel 1:24). Our attention is, therefore, directed to both — "the sufferings of Christ, and the glory that should follow" (1 Peter 1:11).

For this purpose the bullock is appropriate as a sacrificial animal, the picture of one of the four living creatures (Revelation 4:7). There is a Roman coin that bears the picture of a bullock with the meaningful inscription "Can be used for service as well as for sacrifice."

Byssus. The byssus fabric is mentioned for the first time in Genesis 41:42. It was the clothing of honor for righteous Joseph in Egypt: the finest white cotton. Of David, Asaph and his brothers, and Mordecai it is recorded that they wore clothes made of this costly material (1 Chronicles 15:27; 2 Chronicles 5:12; Esther 8:15). In ancient Egypt the mummy wrappings of the kings were made of it. The Israelites brought this bright white, extremely fine fabric with them when they left their bondage in Egypt.

The task and intent of the *Gospel of Luke* is to present our Lord Jesus as the Son of Man in His sinless, holy life. "That holy thing which shall be born" (Luke 1:35). His spotless life as a man is aptly represented by the byssus fabric. Deeply convinced of the rightness of His statement, His earthly judge, Pilate, had to say of Him twice, "I find no fault in this man" (Luke 23:4,14). The purity and righteousness of the defendant left no shadow of a doubt. He was "the righteous one" — as the New Testament calls Him seven times.

In agreement with this, we find the fourth living creature in Revelation with the appearance "of a man." The Faithful and True One, the Man of God in the most truthful sense of the word, could be properly represented only by the pure byssus fabric. Let us think about this each time we find this material mentioned.

God had commanded Moses that his helpers, Bezaleel and Aholiab, who were filled with the Spirit of God, should embroider these four types of textile threads into a unified whole. They carried out the task, and under their hands was produced the wonderful gate hanging, which we are now given to understand as a symbolic presentation of our Savior — He who became man.

When we read Psalm 139, we can only be amazed how the Spirit of God there described the development of a human body. Verses 14 and 15 move us to amazement and adoring joy when we read, "I will praise thee; for I am fearfully and wonderfully made: marvelous are thy works . . . when I was made . . . curiously wrought. . . ."

How surprisingly fitting is this description when we consider the work of those craftsmen who finished the gate hanging in "embroidery." One can almost hear the voice of the incarnate Son of God in those verses of the 139th Psalm. His incarnation was the miracle of all miracles. Therefore the praise of the angel hosts at His birth: "Glory to God in the highest" (Luke 2:14). "And without controversy great is the mystery of godliness: God was manifest in the flesh" (1 Timothy 3:16).

"I am the door; by me if any man enter in, he shall be saved" (John 10:9). Blessed are all who have experienced eternal salvation through Him in that they have in full confidence entered by this unique, wonderful gate. By their trust they glorify the Lord Jesus who is worthy of trust and, at the same time, they obtain for themselves deliverance from the judgment that the godless outside have to face. "Through Him" saved, sheltered — and blessed.

THE HANGINGS OF THE OUTER COURT

Anyone entering the courtyard finds himself totally surrounded by byssus. He sees shining white everywhere, the color of purity — a totally new sight in contrast to what he has hitherto known: the desolate, unclean desert. In this way the visitor experiences a blessed change: once outside, now inside; once far from God, now inside the door, in the realm of the blessing of the Highest.

Today also every sinner who obeys the inviting call of

Sixty pillars, fitted with silver hooks, outlined the courtyard. They were made of acacia wood and were set in sockets of brass. The tops were overlaid with silver. The height of these pillars was 5 cubits.

Jesus Christ in the obedience of faith experiences this change. He takes refuge in Him and is brought by Him into a new relationship to the living God — "who . . . called us with a holy calling, not according to our works, but according to his own . . . grace, which was given us in Christ Jesus"(2 Timothy 1:9).

The Pillars With the Copper Bases and the Silver Capitals

All sixty pillars of the courtyard were made of the same materials. Their bases were of brass, their capitals were overlaid with silver, and the posts were of acacia wood.

There were no instructions designating the material out of which the posts were to be made. There was, however, hardly any other raw material than acacia wood for them to consider, since the rest of the columns and planks of the tabernacle were without exception made of acacia wood, according to the divine instruction.

All the materials of the entire tabernacle should turn our eyes and our hearts to the One, our highly praised Lord. Everything must give testimony to His glory.

The acacia wood is a very beautiful picture of the true humanity of the Son of God. He is the branch out of David's tribe, the sprig and the shoot, as the prophets describe Him (Isaiah 11:1; Jeremiah 23:5,6; Zechariah 6:12). Did He not designate Himself in Luke 23:31 as the "green tree"? Here the Greek phrase for this material, "the incorruptible wood," is precisely correct.

All of this indicates that he was born into this world as the second Adam. He was the "root out of a dry ground," out of spiritually dead Israel (Isaiah 53:2).

The bases of brass remind us of the voluntary suffering of the Lord Jesus. He was "a man of sorrows, and acquainted with grief" (Isaiah 53:3). This extremely fire-resistant metal is a symbol for Him as the One who suffered, was tested, and withstood the judgment.

The silver-overlaid capitals of the pillars remind us that He "gave Himself a ransom for all" (1 Timothy 2:5,6).

It will help us to understand an additional significance of the courtyard pillars if we contemplate the expressions the Holy Spirit uses in Psalm 144:12 and Galatians 2:9. There He likens saved people to pillars. We see here a picture of believers as God has placed them together to be a witness for Jesus Christ in this world.

They are pillars according to their God-given essence and position — they all have the life of Jesus Christ as represented in the acacia wood. The world around can perceive this new life in all true Christians. Sometime and somewhere it is evident to those around us.

Here we would direct special attention to one expression we encounter in 1 John 2:8. In this connection it is of fundamental importance. John witnesses to us of a unique fact with the words "which thing is true in him and in you."

There is, therefore, one nature that the Son of Man manifested on the earth and that became apparent in His disciples through God's grace. Through the second birth everyone who has surrendered to the Lord Jesus Christ is given new, eternal life. These believers are placed as born-again ones in the world. Although *in* the world, they are no longer *of* the world (John 15:19; 17:14). The Cross and the Crucified One separate us from the ungodly principles and from the spirit of this age, whose prince is Satan. Paul attests to this with complete clarity when he says, "But God forbid that I should glory, save in the cross of our Lord Jesus Christ, by whom the world is crucified unto me, and I unto the world" (Galatians 6:14). Nothing could be clearer; there is no room for compromise.

That this also brings distress and suffering was announced by our Lord Himself (John 15:18). So then, with Him we are tested and suffering ones, and for His sake are scorned and reviled. Peter emphasizes this with these important words: "If ye be reproached for the name of Christ, happy are ye; for the spirit of glory and of God resteth upon you. . ." (1 Peter 4:12–16). May God so guard us that there will be no other cause for us to be reviled!

The silver overlay of the pillar capitals reminds us, as if by admonition, of a word of Paul in Ephesians 6:17: "And take the helmet of salvation." Does this not lend a particular dignity to the messenger of the gospel, to strengthen him in this hostile world? Once God called out to the Israelites who had been freed from Pharaoh's yoke: "I am Jehovah your God . . . I have broken the bars of your yoke, and made you go *upright*" (Leviticus 26:13 ASV). How much more does this apply to those who have escaped from the slavery of Satan! Through the Christ of God they rejoice in a glorious freedom. He has broken the yoke of sin and of the law and loosed our bonds (John 8:36; Acts 15:10; Romans 6:18; Galatians 5:1). Christ has freed us for freedom. Therefore our whole life is to be dedicated to Him.

Now let us note the arrangement of the pillars. They were not placed at random here and there, for God is not a God of disorder (1 Corinthians 14:33), but rather in formation, to indicate a definite unity; our Lord and Master so decreed it. Here, for the first time, we see something that was a heartfelt desire of the Son of God as seen in His unique prayer to the Father in John 17: "That they *all* may be *one*." Five times we hear him pray for this. He desires that those who have been entrusted to Him, whom He loves so deeply, present to those about them a testimony worthy of belief. Is that also your wish and mine, and how much are we prepared to sacrifice for it?

The number of pillars also points to this fact. There is a total of sixty (two times three times ten). That could be said to illustrate the following: two is the number of the witnesses; three is the number of the Godhead; ten is the number of human responsibility. The Lord expects of all of us the testimony of unity, which glorifies Him and is enjoined on us as a holy duty.

The White Hangings of Byssus on the Silver Hooks

The rows of pillars all equally supported the white byssus hanging that hung from the silver bars. This byssus is the exalted type of the unspotted righteousness of the Lord Jesus in His earthly life. We want to emphasize the meaning of this fact as strongly as possible, for in Christendom there is a widespread evil teaching about the Christ of God. This heresy presents His humanity as if He had had a part in the sinful nature of Adam. Whoever dares to maintain and teach such a doctrine will not escape the judgment of God.

The white byssus teaches us something totally different. With joy we acknowledge the statements the Holy Spirit so clearly recorded in the Bible. Of our Lord Jesus Christ it is there stated: "And in him is no sin" (1 John 3:5); "who knew no sin" (2 Corinthians 5:21); and "who did no sin, neither was guile found in his mouth" (1 Peter 2:22).

He Himself had faced His enemies and challenged them to declare the truth about Him: "Which of you convicteth me of sin?" (John 8:46 ASV). They all grew silent, full of embarrassment, and raised no accusation against Him.

It is the duty and task of the church of the Lord to hold absolutely to this testimony concerning the spotless and Holy One; otherwise it loses claim to this title of honor and defiles itself with heresy.

This truth is presented by means of the white byssus. It is fundamental to the whole redemptive work of Jesus Christ, for only the Pure can die effectively for the impure, the Righteous for the unrighteous, and the Sinless for the guilty and corrupt. Everything else is satanic distortion of the truth and a blasphemous false doctrine.

"He that is of God heareth the words of God" (John 8:47).

Thus, the byssus, which the sixty pillars of the courtyard supported, declares to us a clear message of Christ's purity. It is at the same time supposed to represent the purity and spotlessness of the witnesses of the assembly of God. What a holy responsibility!

The height of the pillars and the height of the white hanging was five cubits, corresponding to the height of the four-colored hanging of the gate. Five is the number of Christ, the Man dependent upon God. He alone answered fully the requirements of God, to the highest joy of the Father. This is the dimension given to the complete hanging that enclosed the courtyard and shows us what God expects of His redeemed.

The distance between the pillars was likewise five cubits. This may be said to illustrate that our *combined* testimony before the world can be maintained only through faithful dependence on our God. Only genuine obedience born of faith can honor Him. "Finally, brethren, whatsoever things are true, whatsoever things are honest, whatsoever things are just, whatsoever things are pure, whatsoever things are lovely, whatsoever things are of good report; if there be any virtue, and if there be any praise, think on these things" (Philippians 4:8). How impressive are these words for any sincere child of God!

The Pegs of Brass With Their Ropes

Near the upper end of every pillar two silver hooks were attached. One was inside, toward the courtyard, the other outside, facing the opposite direction. On every hook was hung a very strong rope whose free end was fastened to a brass peg, which was driven into the ground one inside the courtyard and one outside for each pillar. This two-sided anchoring insured the immobility of the pillars.

That reminds us of two valuable things that are indispensable for the believer when he wants to stand upright in this world; namely, the daily reading of the Word of God and a faithful prayer life. Both have a healing and sanctifying effect on the life of faith for the child of God. The pegs were of brass, reminding us that Bible reading and prayer should and must lead to self-judgment. When this happens, the testimony of the individual and of the fellowship leads to the glorification of our Lord. "Let the word of Christ dwell in you richly"; "continue in prayer, and watch in the same with thanksgiving" (Colossians 3:16; 4:2). These urgent words of the apostle are an encouragement and earnest exhortation at the same time.

The enclosure made a clear separation between inside and outside. It is the will of our Lord and Master that there should not be any subsequent mixing of the people of God with the children of this world. Surely at all times we owe to the lost a clear and valiant testimony in love and humility, coupled with the invitation to enter through the "door." But Scripture forbids any fellowship with believers who are so in name only, unbelievers, and the godless. Otherwise all church discipline is impossible (2 Corinthians 6:14–18).

The most weighty of accusations, therefore, applied to the negligent assembly in Corinth. "For what have I to do to judge them also that are without? Do not ye judge them that are within? But them that are without God judgeth. Therefore put away from among yourselves that wicked person'' (1 Corinthians 5:12–13).

It is this alone that conforms to the holiness of God and to His just claims on His pardoned church.

WITHIN THE OUTER COURT

The Offerings — The Morning and Evening Burnt Offering

The fire for the sacrifice was lighted here from heaven and was never allowed to be extinguished (Leviticus 6:5–6; 9:22–24). In the early morning of every day, therefore, a blazing fire burned on the brazen altar in the courtyard to consume the sacrifice — a lamb of the first year — for the morning burnt offering. So the Word of God had ordained it in Exodus 29:38–46. The living God desired to be daily honored and satisfied through a burnt offering, morning and evening. In connection with this continual burnt offering, the eternal God declared that the people would be ''sanctified through his glory.'' So this unique offering became a wonderful proof of grace.

In addition, this total offering depicts for us the perfect and undivided dedication of Christ to God. His self-dedication was incomparable and is the eternal basis of all our blessings. The burnt offering was instituted to satisfy the yearning of the very heart of God. It was presented for Him alone. He found delight in the consecration of His Son, who presented Himself in so wonderful a manner to the eternal glory of His God. The fragrant sweet smell of the dedication of Christ as a burnt offering on the cross is for God alone.

The burnt offering reminds us of Hebrews 9:14:

"Christ, who through the eternal Spirit offered himself without spot to God. . . ." This type of offering fire was most holy. It was called the "bread of his God" (Leviticus 3:10,11; 21:21). Shall not this morning and evening offering also admonish our hearts to place the Lord, who gave Himself voluntarily for the glory of God, daily before our eyes and in our hearts in grateful love?

In the "law of the burnt offering" there is a communication, a command of God, that applied only to Aaron and

At the beginning of each day the priests brought the morning burnt offering. This marked the beginning of the holy service in the courtyard. A one-year-old lamb was consumed by the fire of the brazen altar.

his sons. It proclaims that "the burnt-offering shall be on the hearth upon the altar *all night unto the morning;* and the fire of the altar shall be kept burning thereon" (Leviticus 6:8–9 ASV). Here is something striking. In the early morning Aaron and his sons brought forth the commanded morning offering. Subsequently, throughout the whole day every member of the people of God could bring the voluntary burnt offerings and peace offerings, which were then offered under the direction and with the help of the priests (Leviticus 1:1–17; Psalm 66:13,15). At nightfall the general sacrificial service ceased. Now Aaron with his sons came to the altar to slay and burn the evening offering for God.

This offering now lay the whole night on the glowing embers of the brazen altar until the dawn of day.

This highlights and emphasizes in an impressive manner that the satisfaction of God at the sacrificial death of His beloved Son is without end.

When a priestly attitude fills us, our hearts will share the joy of the Father in the consecration of the Son. May the Holy Spirit remind us of it day and night.

This offering will then also lead us to dedicate our life wholly to God, for less cannot satisfy Him.

When the ashes of the offering fell through the brazen grate of the altar, this was the moment when high, clear tones resounded over the camp of Israel as the silver trumpets held by every priest's hand and blown by every priest's mouth announced to all the blessed message: "It is finished!" (Numbers 10:10; John 19:30). What a heavy responsibility this assignment laid upon the priestly family. The priests were daily witnesses of all these happenings in the service of their exalted God.

Whoever is a priest today through God's grace — it is the privilege of all the children of God — is called to take part in this holy service of sacrifice. He will present his worship to God the Father in spirit and truth with a heart full of reverential wonder. God seeks such worshipers. Does your heart rejoice in this? Where could this better happen than at the table of the Lord, at the breaking of bread, where the symbols of His perfect love stand before us?

The Slaughtering of the Sacrificial Animals

In the picture on page 53 we see three men who are bringing animals to be sacrificed. One of them is leading his animal. The second stands before his sacrifice and a priest is standing with him. The Israelite has designated this animal as the one that should die in his place. With the laying of his hands on the head of the animal and the *simultaneous confession of his sins,* he makes the sacrificial animal *one with himself* (Leviticus 5:5). He places, as it were, his guilt upon the animal, which thereby becomes his substitute. This animal, which is laden with a guilt not his own, must be killed with the slaughtering knife by the hand of the offerer. The third man in the picture, who is slaughtering his sheep, is doing exactly that.

What emotional release must have been felt by the guilty one in the fulfillment of this regulation. If the sacrificed animal was a sin offering or trespass offering. The offerer was assured of full forgiveness. Forgiveness is promised nine times in Leviticus 4:20–6:7 to every offerer who brings this sacrifice in faith. What perfect certainty!

If the animal was brought as a *burnt offering,* the assurance of full acceptance with God becomes an integral part of this offering. What a wonderful type of the Lord Jesus! He was sacrificed in our place; now we have been received by God on the merit of this One (Ephesians 1:6).

The same is true of the *peace offering*. Each was "an offering made by fire, of a sweet savour unto the LORD" (Leviticus 1:9; 3:5).

What joy and blessedness we should experience in our hearts, when we apply these types to our beloved Lord!

Jesus Christ — our sin offering and our trespass offering — effects for us a total deliverance from the power of sin, forgiveness of all guilt, and cleansing from every stain.

Jesus Christ — our burnt offering and our peace offering — obtained for us perfect *acceptance* before God and, in addition, peace and *fellowship* with God.

Worship, praise, and thanksgiving be to Him, the Lamb that was slain!

At the offering of the sacrifice, the priest caught the blood and carried it to the brazen altar. There he spread some of the blood on the four horns of the altar and poured out the rest at the base of the altar. Only the priests could perform this ministry. They alone were allowed to carry out the instructions for the God-given use and application of the blood of the offering.

The Aaronic priesthood ceased 1,900 years ago. Since then the children of God have taken his place. For that reason the Holy Spirit wants to communicate to us a recognition of the uniqueness of the blood of Jesus Christ. He reveals to us, therefore, throughout Holy Writ the great value God places on it and deepens within our hearts adoring admiration for the Lamb without spot or blemish.

When the children of God in their priestly service

"None shall appear before me empty" the Lord had commanded. Everyone, therefore, who approached the Lord brought an offering. Only unblemished animals could be offered to the Most High.

honor the blood of the Lord Jesus Christ in joyful worship, they constantly and anew bring pleasure to God the Father and His Son. This blood has an eightfold work of blessing as a result, according to the loving will of God and His decree of grace:

Forgiveness, for it frees the guilty from the burden of sin (Ephesians 1:7);

Cleansing, for it cleanses the defiled from the shame of their sins (Revelation 1:5);

Justification, for it protects the accused from the penalty of the judgment (Romans 5:9);

Peace with God, for it delivers the former enemies of God from the coming wrath (Colossians 1:20);

Salvation, for it frees the prisoners from the power of sin (1 Peter 1:18);

Sanctification, for it does away with the need for those who were lost to make any attempt to attain redemption through good works (Hebrews 13:12);

Redemption, for it rescues the slaves of Satan from his rule (Revelation 5:8–9);

Access to God, for it calls the homeless from the misery of being far from God (Ephesians 2:13).

"Unto you therefore which believe he is precious" (1 Peter 2:7).

THE BRAZEN ALTAR WITH ITS GRATING

The middle of the courtyard is occupied by the brazen altar. The altar stands on an elevation that could remind us of the "mountain of God" (Ezekiel 26:16) and of Golgotha. The fact that the altar of burnt offering and its horns were of brass demands our attention. This unique

construction of the altar was prescribed for this special place. On other occasions God had allowed an altar made of earth or of stones (Exodus 20:24–25; Deuteronomy 27:5).

Not only were the innumerable offerings that were brought to the altar a type of the Savior, but the altar itself also displays specific details that foreshadowed the glory of the Lord Jesus Christ.

The great significance of this altar is seen in the fact that God names it seventy-seven times. It is remarkable that the Lord Jesus said that the altar, in its typical meaning, is more important than the offering (Matthew 23:19). The brazen altar was called "most holy" by God (Exodus 29:37). We must, therefore, examine it closely. It consisted of the sides, the grating, and the two carrying bars.

The Materials

Four boards of acacia wood comprised the *edging* or the outer framework. In this symbolism we see the incarnation of the Son of God, "born of a woman, born under the Law": "Christ, the Man of God."

This wood was overlaid inside and out with brass, the type of divine righteousness and holiness, in contrast to the sinner and sin. Brass resists the blazing flames of the all-consuming fire, a picture of how our Lord Jesus willingly and submissively bore the fury of God's wrath, yet in singular determination and with incomparable endurance. For this may He be adored!

The grating concealed inside the brazen altar was entirely of brass. The wood with the sacrifice lay directly on it. The oxygen of the inflowing air had free access from beneath. The hottest blaze was concentrated there and remained hidden from the eyes of the priests.

There was indescribable misery in the suffering and death of the Lord Jesus Christ. It was the dreadful endurance of the wrath of God, which no human is able to comprehend. Only the eye and heart of God saw the depth of it. Only God Himself could rightly evaluate this voluntary dedication, this terrible suffering and endurance. It was surely for this reason that God allowed thick darkness to engulf the Cross and the Crucified One during these hours. No eye of man might look upon the holy countenance of this Miserable One, His face disfigured by the judgment of God and by deepest suffering! How profoundly all this should stir our hearts — we who are guilty of the death of this Just One, who as our substitute had to suffer so much! He is worthy of our total love.

The brazen grating lay inside the side boards of the altar, one and a half cubits above the ground, thus being of the same height as the table of shewbread and the ark of the covenant. Is not this a significant harmony? On the altar we see the suffering Christ, on the table the fruit of His suffering, and in the ark the witness of His glory (Exodus 25:10; 27:1,5).

The Framing of the Altar

The height of the *sides* came to three cubits. That may be said to signify that the just claims of the holiness of the Most High must be satisfied. The Crucified One met these claims and fully satisfied God (Hebrews 9:14). Christ *offered Himself to God* through the eternal Spirit.

The width of each of the four boards was five cubits. It means a wonderful assurance for the believer: his distress is ended by the death of the Savior and the demands of God upon Him are irrevocably fulfilled through His death. Five is the number of man dependent on God. As such the Redeemer gave Himself for us. The four sides, the four corners, and the four horns of the altar testify to us that the Good News applies to all sinners in every place, to all races and peoples. It has world-wide significance, as seen in the words of the Risen One: "Go ye into all the world, and preach the gospel to every creature" (Mark 16:15). How we rejoice at this! The saving message of His eternal redemption is to be taken to all

points of the compass. Are we acting as His messengers? If we are silent, we are guilty (2 Kings 7:9 ASV).

The Side Plates

Originally, the brass outer walls of the brazen altar were smooth and polished. For years they remained unchanged until the rebellion of Korah and his followers brought the judgment of God down on them. When the wilderness wanderings began, Korah, a descendant of Levi, was, as a Kohathite, selected by the grace of God with his brethren to carry the covered, most holy vessels of pure gold (Numbers 4:4–20). A worthy service for the Lord!

But Korah was not satisfied with this special privilege; he sought after the high office of the priesthood. As a punishment, he, along with the 250 rebels who followed

The offerer, in laying his hands on the head of the sacrifice and confessing his sin, identified himself with his offering. After that, he had to kill the bound animal with his own hands, using the sacrificial knife.

him, encountered the condemnation of the wrath of God (Numbers 16). These insurgents had come before the Lord audaciously and sacrilegiously with brazen incense censers. Struck dead by the fire of God, they let their censers fall to the ground. At the command of the Lord, Eleazar, the son of Aaron, gathered these brazen censers and hammered each one into a flat plate. These plates were then attached to the sides of the brazen altar in plain view. Every Israelite was for all time solemnly and earnestly warned by this not to strive high-handedly for the office and ministry of the priest.

It is a sad characteristic of name-only Christendom that innumerable men usurp the priestly honor without meeting the requirements that God has ordained beforehand. We read of this rebellion of Korah in Jude 11.

The requirements for the true office of priest today are: to be saved and cleansed by the blood of Jesus Christ (1 Peter 1:18; Revelation 1:5–6), to be born again by the incorruptible seed of the Word of God (1 Peter 1:22–23), and to be sealed by the Holy Spirit (Ephesians 1:12–14). Only those who meet these qualifications — those who are reconciled, made alive, and anointed — may worship God by the Spirit of God (Philippians 3:3).

The Horns of the Altar

The horns of the altar are a picture of strength and stability. Perhaps Zacharias, the priest, was thinking of this when he spoke in his prayer and praise of the "horn of salvation" (Luke 1:69). David had already sung of it in Psalm 18:2.

The priests smeared the blood of the slain offering on these horns of the altar as a testimony to the lasting worth

The brazen altar in the courtyard. Its four sides were of acacia wood completely covered with brass. On the four corners were the brazen horns. The height of the grate was only half that of the sides: one and one-half cubits. The rings on the altar bore the carrying staves.

of the blood. The four horns on the four corners tell us that this good news applies to all sinners. The mouth of God prophetically declared of the Messiah in Isaiah 49:6: "It is a light thing that thou shouldest be my servant to raise up the tribes of Jacob, and to restore the preserved of Israel: I will also give thee for a light to the Gentiles, that thou mayest be my salvation unto the end of the earth."

At that time, a guilty Israelite could lay hold of the horns when he sought refuge. But he experienced deliverance only when he came with a pure heart, with the confession of his trespass, and with faith. Joab and Adonijah are examples of men today who, as religious formalists, expect salvation from the sacraments without a change of heart. All such have fallen into a terrible delusion and will reap judgment in spite of the sacraments. Then as now, the divine requirement of complete sincerity applied to everyone (1 Kings 1:49–53; 2:28–34). "Blessed is the man . . . in whose spirit there is no guile" (Psalm 32:2).

The Two Carrying Staves

The two carrying staves were of acacia wood covered with brass. They depict for us two wonderful characteristics of our great Savior and Redeemer. He is both *Reconciler* and *Savior.* He is Reconciler in view of God's claim against the hostile sinner: ". . . that he may make peace with me; and he shall make peace with me" (Isaiah 27:5). There was only one Person to whom this applies: "The chastisement of our peace was upon him" (Isaiah 53:5). He "made peace through the blood of his cross" (Colossians 1:20). He "came and preached peace to you which were afar off, and to them that were nigh" (Ephesians

2:17). *Eight times* the New Testament speaks of the fact that the believer is reconciled to God (Romans 5:10; 2 Corinthians 5:18–20; Colossians 1:21). Because the guilt of sin separates the natural man from God, the question of atonement is of such great importance. "He is the propitiation for our sins" (1 John 2:2). How this assurance fills our hearts with the joy of salvation: "Blessed is the people that know the joyful sound"; "thou shalt compass me about with songs of deliverance" (Psalm 89:15; 32:7).

God be praised, for Jesus Christ is also our Savior! Three powers held us captive by their spell: Satan, original sin, and death. The power of Satan rules over the sinner (Acts 26:18). Sin produces evil desire in him, and its power compels him to do that which is evil (Romans 7:8,13,17). Death rules over all the descendants of Adam and exacts its tribute (Romans 5:14). The chains of this miserable slavery could be broken only by One Person: the Victor, Christ Jesus our Lord. He brought us freedom, for Satan has been conquered, the power of sin broken, and death overcome. Glory and honor are due Him, the glorious Liberator!

THE BRAZEN LAVER WITH ITS STAND

Between the brazen altar and the tabernacle stood a unique vessel — the brazen laver. Its very position is of significant and fundamental importance. Probably men would have assigned it another place, but the mouth of God ordained the location. Thus, according to the opinion of men, a wash basin should stand up front at the entrance or even before the gate. This view rests on the assumption that the sinner had every reason to cleanse himself before entering the courtyard. Only when he is washed and clean can he enter the presence of God!

These people do not reflect, however, that the lost person cannot approach God through personal effort, but he can do so only by means of an offering, which becomes his substitute and atones for him and his guilt. Only with such an offering can he stand before a holy and just God. Once he has made this blood offering, he is fully justified (Hebrews 10:10,14; 13:12; Romans 3:23–26).

The altar of burnt offering is the place where the sinner comes into a new relationship with God and is placed in a new position of blessing before Him. This position cannot be lost (Romans 5:19). God be praised for it!

The one so justified and sanctified is made worthy and is called to conscious fellowship with the living God. But this fellowship requires a sanctification lived out in practice, that is, the endeavor to match the position given by grace with a life of faith. What is more, this sanctification that is required of the saved is possible. "But like as he who called you is holy, be ye yourselves also holy in all manner of living" (1 Peter 1:15 ASV). How does this sanctification come about? It is made possible through "the washing of water by the word" (Ephesians 5:26). Such is the service of love of the Lord Jesus Christ to all children of God.

The great multitude of redeemed priests involves,

therefore, a most holy obligation: to expose heart and mind daily to the cleansing work of the Word of God. Only in this manner can one speak of a true fellowship with the Father and with the Son. It is a wonderful calling for all children of God and results in "full joy" (1 John 1:3–4).

Therefore, the position of the laver is correctly chosen: not before, but *beyond* the brazen altar.

Can we ever forget that the Lord Jesus washed the feet of His disciples before He went to Gethsemane? As Peter learned at that time, so we learn what the washing of the feet implies, namely, that we have a part with Jesus, true fellowship with Him. That fellowship is what His loving heart yearns for. What effect does this knowledge have on you and me? (John 13:8).

The priest in the picture on page 63 has already washed his feet and cleansed his hands. He is drying them in order to carry out his service. The water carrier is not a priest, as his clothes show. We assume that he belongs to the Nethinim, the "gifted ones," who served as temple servants. They were entrusted to Aaron (1 Chronicles 9:2). Seventeen times they are named in the Word of God. We should not esteem them or their service unimportant.

We who are children of God are given to our High Priest, Jesus Christ, by the Father, to serve Him in faithfulness and self-denial. Do we not hear the joy in His own words when He designates us as those whom the Father gave to Him? Seven times in John 17 He so designates the saved children of God. Is this not an all-surpassing joy?

We seek the dimensions of the laver in the Holy Scriptures in vain. Why did God not give us any kind of measurement? We will understand it when we consider

The cleansing that God required of the priests took place at the laver. The servants of the Holy One were required to wash their hands and feet before every service they performed at the altar or in the tent; otherwise they risked the penalty of death.

that the basin that is filled with water typifies the Word of God. Psalm 119:96 states, "But Thy commandment is exceeding broad." This is the reason why there is no mention of a limit of any kind. No mortal has ever exhausted the fullness of the Word of God, even in a long life of faith — it is immeasureable.

The material for the laver was wholly of brass. This metal portrays the inexorable judgment of divine testing. Moses received the metal hand mirrors as offerings from the women of the people of Israel for the making of the laver (Exodus 38:8). With what pleasure the eyes of God rested upon the pious daughters and mothers who gave such expression to their self-denial and consecration. They demonstrated clearly by this that their service for God meant more than the cultivation of vanity. They wanted to contribute unreservedly to equipping the house of God in a fitting manner. Is there something of this spirit among us?

The mirrors of the women and the reflecting surface of the water in the laver are alike reminders of an appropriate word in James, who described the Word of God as a mirror. "But be ye doers of the Word, and not hearers only, deceiving your own selves." We are called upon to look into this mirror and to continue looking into it to become blessed doers of the Word (James 1:22–25).

The laver was filled with spring water. Was this not water from the smitten rock, which was a special gift of God? (Exodus 17:3,6; 1 Corinthians 10:4). True, the water from the rock was intended first of all to quench the tormenting thirst of the people of God. But where did the priests obtain the water that was brought for personal washing and for the washing of the parts of the slain

offerings? The Lord had ordained both (Exodus 29:17; Leviticus 1:9,13).

The stand of brass supported the laver and held it and its contents up from the earth, for the Word of God is not earthly, but heavenly. Therefore, "see that ye refuse not him that speaketh . . . from heaven" (Hebrews 12:25). With godly authority His message is directed to our hearts. Only those who follow the Lord in the obedience of faith out of thankful love can respond aright to this call.

The Cleansing of the Priests

The cleansing of the priests, the washing of their hands and feet, was a particularly strict commandment of the Lord. It is also seen in the fact that the omission of this cleansing was punished with death. "For Aaron and his sons shall wash their hands and their feet thereat: when they go into the tabernacle of the congregation . . . when they come near to the altar to minister . . . that they die not: and it shall be a statute for ever" (Exodus 30:17–21).

What holy solemnity lies in these words! They are the expression of the words of God: ". . . ye shall be holy; for

The laver, as well as its stand, was made of brass. It stood between the brazen altar and the tabernacle. Out of the smitten rock flowed the stream of water, and from it this basin was constantly refilled.

I am holy. . . ." *Seven times* God says this to His servants (Leviticus 11:44; cf. 1 Peter 1:16).

Like the brazen altar, the laver is also called "most holy" (Exodus 30:29). That this basin is mentioned *ten times* shows us once again the responsibility that lies on all the priests of God: the experience of daily sanctification, represented by the cleansing in the laver. Is that not in the words of the Lord Jesus as He prayed to the Father for you and me: "Sanctify them through thy truth: thy word is truth" (John 17:17). How deeply all this must impress us!

We are "perfected for ever" "by one offering" (Hebrews 10:14), and to us apply the words "Finally, brethren, farewell. Be perfect . . ." and "that the man of God may be perfect, thoroughly furnished unto all good works" (2 Corinthians 13:11; 2 Timothy 3:17).

The Prayer of the Priests

Prayer is one of the most exalted acts to which every priest was to be "fully suited" and prepared. This presupposes a heart, however, that is filled with trust in Almighty God. But not only that. If prayer is to be heard, there is another important prerequisite, which we find in 1 Timothy 2:8: "I will therefore that men pray every where, lifting up holy hands. . . ." This refers to the works we do with our hands. They must correspond to the will of God if we want to be sure that our prayers will be answered.

The commandment of the Lord applies to all priests today, to diligently use the laver to cleanse themselves.

"For Aaron and his sons shall wash their hands . . . thereat" (Exodus 30:19). Do we understand this symbolic

language and its meaning? Brethren — are we priests with clean hands? Or is our prayer restrained perhaps through hidden sin, which we need to confess before God and man, before we can practice a ministry before God with a clear conscience?

"Who shall stand in his holy place? He that hath clean hands, and a pure heart" (Psalm 24:3–4). And: "The priests and the Levites were purified together, all of them were pure" (Ezra 6:20). Blessed pray-ers!

Obviously, it is expected not only of believing men that they pray, even though public prayer in the church is their responsibility and their general privilege (1 Corinthians 14:34–37). But godly praying women are an invaluable help outside the assembly of the saints, for example, at home and in the family, if no man is present, and also among children and women in the ministry of missions and in children's work. Their supplication and prayer ministry is indispensable and of great worth. When they persevere before the face of God with covered heads, streams of blessings will follow in all that they do (1 Corinthians 11:3–10).

Let us recall Hannah, the mother of Samuel, and Anna, the prophetess of the tribe of Asher (1 Samuel 1:9–18; Luke 2:36–38). The example of these two women in particular is of very great importance. Where are the women and girls who will imitate them? You faithful sisters, God bless you!

"They shall wash their feet thereat." Do not these words remind us that our walk, our daily association with people, our neighbors, must please God," that [our] prayers be not hindered"? (1 Peter 3:7). God heard the prayer of Cornelius because of his piety and because of his acts of love (Acts 10:4). "The effectual fervent prayer of a *righteous man* availeth much" (James 5:16).

Another encouraging example is that married couple of the priestly race in a city in the mountains of Judah. Concerning them, the Word of God records what God expects of all believing married couples: "And they were both righteous before God, walking in all commandments and ordinances of the Lord blameless." God's pleasure rested upon them. He therefore sent His messenger to deliver the message of comfort and encouragement to the husband during his priestly service as he persevered in prayer: "Fear not, Zacharias: for thy prayer is heard" (Luke 1:5–13).

3. The Tabernacle Structure

THE EXTERIOR OF THE TABERNACLE

We come now to the actual tent of meeting, the tabernacle of the living God.

All that we have seen in the courtyard serves solely to make sinful men acceptable to appear in the holy presence of the Most High through the wonderful grace of God. Once this happened, the decrees of His eternal love could find fulfillment.

The indispensable prerequisite for this was the work of reconciliation, redemption, and sanctification. People, having "been made sinners," needed to "be made righteous." "But where sin abounded, grace did much more abound" (Romans 5:19–20). Grace shows itself in the fact that common people became holy priests, who were able to fulfill with insight and devotion the requirements of a holy God. The redeeming work of Jesus on the cross is the unique, wonderful prerequisite for all this.

But the redeemed are presented here not only in the figure of the priesthood, but also as "an holy temple in the Lord: in whom ye also are builded together for an habitation of God through the Spirit" (Ephesians 2:20–22), "whose house are we" (Hebrews 3:6). "Know ye not that ye are the temple of God, and that the Spirit of God

The tent of meeting, the sanctuary of the Lord, was veiled with four coverings. The outer two coverings of skin were stretched in the fashion of a tent. They provided working space and living quarters for the priests.

dwelleth in you?'' (1 Corinthians 3:16). Let us think about this as we consider together the particulars of this dwelling place of God.

The tabernacle did not have any solid ceilings as is customary in our houses — no beams of wood, no walls of stone. The tent of meeting was built like a tent, as its name indicates, and was covered with four coverings. Two coverings of skins and two of woven carpeting enclosed the tabernacle.

THE COVERING OF BADGERS' SKINS

The appearance of this covering was not attractive. Inconspicuous and dull in color, it was not an arresting sight for passersby. The badgers' skins did not arouse the covetousness of the surrounding peoples. Like many other details of the tabernacle, this covering is a portrait of the incarnate Son of God, Jesus Christ. The prophet Isaiah described Him with these beautifully fitting words: ''He hath no form nor comeliness; and when we shall see him, there is no beauty that we should desire him'' (Isaiah 53:2). His appearance was so unimpressive that John says of Him three times: ''And the world knew him not. . . . There standeth one among you, whom ye know not. . . . And I knew him not . . .'' (John 1:10,26,31). Among His fellow citizens He was mostly known as the ''carpenter'' — a simple craftsman — he meant nothing more to them (Mark 6:3). He took upon Himself the form of a servant (Philippians 2:7). God, through the prophet Isaiah, calls Him ''my servant'' seven times. This designation spoken by God has a wonderful ring to the ear of the believer. It tells us of the infinite pleasure and holy joy of the Father in the Son.

The second thing that this covering may signify concerns a characteristic peculiarity of the animal from which it originates. The badger is known as a loner. It lives alone; it is not a herd animal.

We hear the voice of our Lord and Savior in the words of Psalm 25:16: "Turn thee unto me, and have mercy upon me; for I am desolate and afflicted." Five times in the Gospels we read of Him that He was alone. Lastly, He had to tell His disciples with grief of heart: "Behold, the hour cometh . . . that ye . . . shall leave me alone" (John 16:32). His singular joy was, as we hear it three times from His mouth: "I am not alone, because the Father is with me" (John 8:16,29; 16:32).

At the same time, His solitude among men was a symbol of holy separation, as it is written of Him: ". . . who is holy, harmless, undefiled, separate from sinners" (Hebrews 7:26). Although filled with deep, incomparable love for the sinner, He nevertheless held Himself constantly apart from their evil ways and deeds.

This covering may have still a third meaning. It lies in this, that the badger is extremely vigilant. This too was a characteristic of the Lord Jesus Christ. He jealously protected the laws of God so they would not be impugned or thwarted. That brought Him into bitter hostility with those people who placed human rules upon the people of God. By these human rules the claims of God were rendered inoperative (Matthew 15:1–20). These men offended the laws of God with their traditions. We know the expression of holy wrath: "The zeal of thine house hath eaten me up" (John 2:17).

These three typical features are represented in the covering of badgers' skins. We see in them once again the divine statement, which here and later (with the other coverings of the tabernacle) can be applied to all the redeemed: "Which thing is true in him and in you" (1 John 2:8). The fact that the covering belongs to the house of God clearly shows us that these attributes of the Lord Jesus Christ should, according to the thoughts of God, be applied to His church. We are obligated to do so. If the assembly of God is to be like the Lord Jesus Christ in this world, it must remain inconspicuous and not expect any recognition from its environment. It will be misunderstood and scorned. Yet for His church, it is enough to be known and loved by the Lord.

At the same time the assembly of God is also filled with a holy vigilance, as Paul expressed it: "For I am jealous over you with godly jealousy" (2 Corinthians 11:2). The claims of God should always be fully recognized in the church's life of faith. When men scorn the directions and commands of the Lord for His assembly or church and introduce their own statutes, they make themselves liable to divine judgment. The teaching of the Lord Jesus Christ is always threatened in this world, because the enemy never sleeps. That requires a spiritual determination in the faithful to hold fast and defend the entire unchanging truth in love. "Watch ye, stand fast in the faith, quit you like men, be strong" (1 Corinthians 16:13). "And what I say unto you I say unto all, Watch" (Mark 13:37). "Blessed are those servants, whom the Lord when he cometh shall find watching" (Luke 12:37).

Is it by chance that the Holy Scriptures voice the call fourteen times: "Watch!" The covering of badgers' skins reminds us of this. God did not specify the dimensions for this veil, which was to cover the entire tabernacle. This should lead us to ponder the fact that He expects from us faithfulness and separation from every manner of evil all the time (1 Thessalonians 5:22). There is no limit to the need for watchfulness and determination and spiritual zeal.

Are we ready to measure our life and the condition of our church by this requirement and to make the necessary changes?

Are not the characteristics of the covering of badgers' skins impressive?

THE COVERING OF RAMS' SKINS

Valuable thoughts present themselves in the contemplation of the second covering of the tabernacle, the covering of rams' skins. The ram was the sacrifice for the consecration of the priests (Exodus 29:1,31). It was a ram that Abraham was told to offer in the place of Isaac (Genesis 22:13). This animal is a picture of energy and vitality. It is the ram that leads the flock.

The life of the Lord Jesus was characterized by a perfect

and completely dedicated consecration to God. This consecration was coupled with a powerful spiritual energy that marked Him as the leader of His group. Was He not the faithful representative of the One of whom the covering of rams' skins was only a picture?

Dedication to His God permeated Jesus' entire earthly existence. Everything that was in accord with the pleasure of the Father. The Lord Jesus did or spoke out of the profoundest feelings of His heart. He could say in truth, "I delight to do thy will, O my God" (Psalm 40:8). The heart's desire of this One who was continually dedicated to God was expressed in the words "There is none upon earth that I desire beside thee" (Psalm 73:25) and "Make me to go in the path of thy commandments; for therein do I delight" (Psalm 119:35).

Heaven could therefore open upon Him, and for this reason the Father could say, "This is my beloved Son, in whom I am well pleased" (Matthew 3:17). Do we have the same joy in the Son of God as the Father has?

The red-dyed rams' skins point to the fact that the Son did not shrink from the ultimate — the sacrifice of His life. "He . . . became obedient unto death, even the death of the cross" (Philippians 2:8). Nothing could dissuade Him. A holy energy marked all His actions, as shown in the words "Therefore have I set my face like a flint" (Isaiah 50:7). His disciples were witnesses of it as He "stedfastly set his face to go to Jerusalem" (Luke 9:51). Soon thereafter they heard Him say, "Arise, let us go hence" (John 14:31). And then they went to Gethsemane. How this touches our hearts!

Should not His holy example impress the words of Romans 12:1 upon us: ". . . that ye present your bodies a

living sacrifice, holy, acceptable unto God, which is your reasonable service"?

In addition, the rams' skins remind us of the fact that God exalted His chosen One to be "Prince and a Savior" (Acts 5:31). God had previously announced Him as a "Governor, that shall rule my people Israel" (Matthew 2:6). Faithful to this task, He led His flocks to graze. In the hour of danger He placed Himself protectively before His disciples and said to His enemies: "If therefore ye seek

me, let these go their way" (John 18:8). Therefore He could say to the Father, "Those that thou gavest me I have kept, and none of them is lost" (John 17:12).

The Lord Jesus is also a leading example to all who allow themselves to be used of Him, that they "take heed . . . to all the flock" (Acts 20:28) as overseers during the time of His absence, and that they insist on the claims of God with spiritual energy and vitality.

The eleven-part curtain of goats' hair and the four-colored cherubim covering.

"Where no counsel is, the people fall . . ." (Proverbs 11:14). For the faithful among them awaits the "crown of glory that fadeth not away" (1 Peter 5:4). Where overseers of the church fulfill their responsibility in this way, there the work of God will grow. Leaders are men who are characterized by spiritual energy and determination. These are the qualities Peter wishes not only for those who bear the responsibility but for every brother. They are proof of a genuine faith life (2 Peter 1:3,5).

Also with the red-colored rams' skins no dimensions are given. The meaning of this is the same as with the badgers' skins.

THE COVERING OF GOATS' HAIR

"A prophet shall the Lord your God raise up unto you of your brethren, like unto me; him shall ye hear in all things . . ." (Acts 3:22). With these words Peter cites the prophecy of Moses, applying it with absolute clarity to the Messiah.

The material for the covering. In the covering of goats' hair we are reminded of the garment and the appearance of the prophets. Elijah was clothed with a coat of hair and was recognized by it (2 Kings 1:8). False prophets sought to make their false prophecies believable by wearing such clothing (Zechariah 13:4). The religious Jews of Jesus' time looked for the Christ of God. They thought John was possibly the Christ and asked, "Art thou *that prophet?*" (John 1:21,25). This unique Person did not appear until that time. They were still expecting Him.

In the New Testament the Lord Jesus is called a "prophet" *fifteen times.* He is seen and heard in this capacity in the Gospels. A great part of His message is made up of prophetic pronouncements. The people who trustingly listened to Him were therefore right in saying, "A great prophet is risen up among us; and . . . God hath visited his people" (Luke 7:16).

The goats' hair for the covering of the tabernacle was spun by God-fearing women. Working with their hands, they prepared this fabric with loving care, for the glory of God (Exodus 35:26). This is mentioned seven times. These women were like the women who followed the Lord and "ministered unto him of their substance" (Luke 8:1–3).

The covering of goats' hair is called "the tent" in the divine record. That reminds us that it is said of the Son of God: "And the Word was made flesh and dwelt [Greek, 'tented'] among us, and we beheld his glory . . ." (John 1:14).

The dimensions of the covering. Every band of the covering measured three times ten cubits in length. In the number three we recognize the divine Trinity; the number ten expresses the responsibility of man before God. We are also reminded here of the Lord Jesus, who in His function as prophet fulfilled His responsibility before God to the fullest degree. His prophetic ministry embraces the whole world, as expressed by the number four. Every band of the covering was four cubits wide.

If we understand the symbolic language of the numbers in the Bible we will be reassured by a knowledge of the four Gospels, for there we will see how "the true and faithful witness" was untiringly and continuously active. His love for the Father motivated Him to be so, "for he whom God hath sent speaketh the words of God" (John

3:34). "I must work the works of him that sent me, while it is day: the night cometh, when no man can work" (John 9:4).

Twenty-eight times in the Holy Scriptures the he-goat is mentioned as a sin offering. The he-goat directs our attention to a fact that moves our hearts and is of the highest importance; by it we are reminded of the event that took place on the cross. There our beloved Savior gave Himself freely "to be sin for us" (2 Corinthians 5:21).

Through the sin-energized nature we inherited from Adam, we would have been eternally separated from God. This nature would never have allowed union between God and us. The result would have been eternal perdition for us, a future full of terror, horror, and despair.

This terrible destiny could be averted only by the incomparable, once-for-all sin offering of the Lord Jesus. This covering of goats' hair is a witness of that fact for us. If we allow the offering of Jesus to speak thus to us, our hearts will be moved to worshipful thanksgiving.

Two panels — one composed of five, and one of six bands — sewn together along the long sides, were fastened by fifty clasps of brass, so that the instructions of God would be carried out: "that it may be one" (Exodus 26:11).

Through a closer study of this arrangement we can see in this part of the tabernacle — as in the wonderful house itself — a striking picture of the church of Jesus Christ. In this the God-desired unity of the assembly of God clearly comes to expression. We know that the number fifty speaks of unification. The fiftieth year, the year of jubilee, reunites that which had become torn apart and separated in the previous fifty years (Leviticus 25:10). At the feeding of the five thousand the Lord commanded that the people should *sit together* in groups of fifty (Luke 9:14). Fifty days after the resurrection of the Lord Jesus Christ the Holy Spirit united the scattered children of God *into a unified whole* (John 11:52).

These facts speak clearly enough to convince us that God desires *the visible unity of believers* — never, however, at the expense of the truth. For that reason the two panels had to be fastened together with brass clasps. The righteous claims of God must always be maintained, and the brass symbolizes the uncompromising righteousness of a holy God and the judgment Christ bore — a judgment that preceded unification.

The covering of goats' hair also reminds us that even in the New Testament church of the Lord there was to be an active prophetic ministry.

What the apostle Paul wrote to the church at Corinth tells us something of it. In his first letter to them he wrote seven times of prophesying. That applies to all Christians: "Wherefore, brethren, covet to prophesy" (1 Corinthians 14:1,3,39).

Eleven individual panels, connected together to form one large covering, are a suggestion that this prophetic ministry should be carried out not only as the obligation and responsibility of the brethren. Much rather, God expects that it will occur in unconstrained, blessed spontaneity — out of love to the saints. How valuable and helpful it is then!

"Even so ye, forasmuch as ye are zealous of spiritual gifts, seek that ye may *excel* to the edifying of the church" (1 Corinthians 14:12).

Are you — are we — prepared for this?

If this service is to have the effect that God desires and is to bring lasting fruit, it is absolutely necessary that brethren who minister exercise continuing self-judgment. The clasps of brass are a reminder of this. If this exercise of heart under the discipline of the Holy Spirit is absent, there is the danger that instead of uniting and bringing together the children of God, there will be a sinful scattering into interest groups. The apostle Paul alluded to this tragic possibility in Acts 20:30: "Of your own selves shall men arise, speaking perverse things, to draw away disciples after them." The history of Christendom gives sufficient evidence of such cases; they are a great shame to us. In deep sorrow the very same servant of God was later obliged to write to the Philippians: "For all seek their own, not the things which are Jesus Christ's" (2:21).

THE FOUR-COLORED CHERUBIM COVERING

The innermost covering of the "golden house" was the cherubim covering. It is striking and highly impressive, as is fitting for its significance.

The divine record begins with the statement "Moreover thou shalt make the tabernacle[1] with ten curtains of fine twined linen, and blue, and purple, and scarlet: with cherubims of cunning work shalt thou make them" (Exodus 26:1–6). Does not the fact that God calls it ninety-nine times His "dwelling" clearly show us how highly He treasures His tabernacle, which was decorated with this covering?

[1]The German translation here uses the word *dwelling* for "tabernacle."

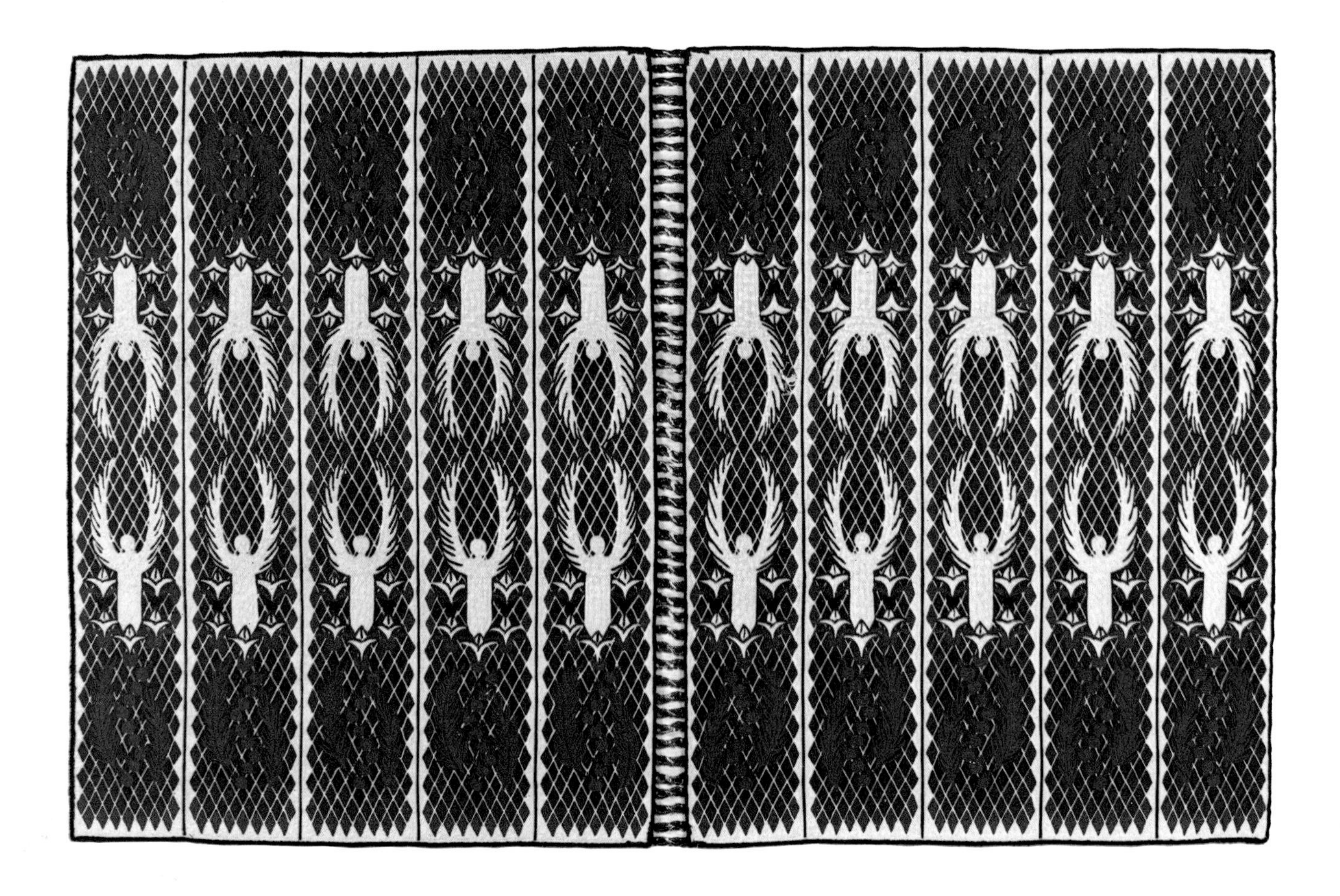

The Lord Jesus once spoke of Himself and His holy body as "this temple" (John 2:19,20). God dwelt at that time in a pure, unspotted human body. Since the completion of the work of salvation, the glory of God has continued to dwell on the earth. But now His dwelling place is in a Being, whom the Holy Spirit characterizes with a unique name: "The Christ" (1 Corinthians 1:6,13; 12:12). In the letters of the New Testament He reveals, through the apostle Paul, this truth and blessed reality, which had been hidden until then. It is a secret of a peculiar type that was made known to Paul by divine revelation; this is why Paul had a special understanding of the "mystery of Christ," the administration and proclamation of which was entrusted to him (Ephesians 3:3–4,9).

"The unsearchable riches of Christ" — that is what one would wish most to write under the picture above, for it is in actuality a wonderful presentation of the riches of Christ, insofar as any picture can adequately express them (Ephesians 3:8).

The ten-part cherubim curtain was named "the dwelling place." It was the innermost covering of the golden house. The embroidery was done in the four familiar colors that are so often mentioned: white byssus, blue, purple, and scarlet. Each strip of the curtain was 28 cubits long and 4 cubits wide. Fifty gold clasps, suspended in blue eyelets fastened the two halves of the curtain together. Each band bore the image of two cherubim.

The colors, materials, and measurements all speak of this richness. This should lead us to consider once again the words of 1 John 2:8: ". . . which thing is true in him and in you." Four glorious attributes of our Lord Jesus Christ are clearly recognizable in the four colors. Since we have already considered them in the description of the gate hanging of the outer court, they are familiar to us.

The white byssus is here named in the divine record for the first time. The Spirit of God clearly attaches the highest value to exalting the spotless humanity of the Savior. This is the foundation and prerequisite for His work of salvation. Only One who is sinless could die as a substitute for sinners and effect their eternal salvation, "the just for the unjust" (1 Peter 3:18).

The blue presents to us the Heavenly One, the Son of God. The purple shows us that He is the King of Kings, and the scarlet-colored yarn speaks of the offering of the blood of the suffering servant, through which He wrought forgiveness and cleansing for us.

The Lord bestows this glorious quality on His beloved redeemed ones. What applies to the Head of the body is also by divine grace true of His body, the assembly of God. Everything points to their new God-given position in Jesus Christ. They are *the justified ones,* holy and blameless before Him (Ephesians 1:1,4). They are named *the heavenly ones* (1 Corinthians 15:48) who are blessed in heavenly places and put in the heavenly places with Him (Ephesians 1:3; 2:6). Of them it is testified that they have become a *kingdom* and a royal priesthood (Revelation 1:6; 5:10). They are made worthy to suffer with Him and to die for Him (Philippians 1:20,29). *The fellowship of His sufferings* will one day produce an indescribable joy at the revelation of His glory (Philippians 3:10; 1 Peter 4:13).

The colors are all wonderfully woven together. They form an embroidery. Only for the ephod of the priest's garment and for the inner veil does God prescribe this style of work. It reveals something of the incomparable beauty of the whole: Christ and His church, a miracle of the grace of God!

The cherubim forms woven into this covering have a specific meaning. When Aaron and his sons went into the tabernacle and looked up, they saw these pictures of heavenly beings. It is not difficult to see that these cherubim forms relate to a divine message concerning the church, namely, "to the intent that now unto the principalities and powers in heavenly places might be known by the church the manifold wisdom of God, according to the eternal purpose which he purposed in Christ Jesus our Lord" (Ephesians 3:10,11).

We do well indeed if we continually keep this fact before us. It will cause us to conduct ourselves in our gatherings as a church in a manner pleasing to God and becoming to us. We are continually observed by the hosts of God. Consequently, the believing woman should have her head covered in the church, "because of the angels" (1 Corinthians 11:10); they would otherwise be shocked by the disobedience of the women. In the same manner, believing men should never attempt to pray with their heads covered, since they are the image and glory of God (1 Corinthians 11:7).

The divine ordinance regarding the cherubim forms in the covering "of the dwelling" is strange and yet characteristic. We involuntarily think of what Peter informs us, namely, that "angels desire to look into" these relationships (1 Peter 1:12).

Two sets — each of five curtains — were sewn together along their long sides and so they comprise two panels. These two panels were permanently held together by fifty golden clasps, each end of which was inserted in one of the fifty blue eyes or loops, that it should "be *one* tabernacle" (Exodus 26:6). So declares the divine direction here as with the goats' hair covering.

This binding together reminds us — as the clear teaching in Ephesians 2:11–18 shows — of the two groups that are joined together through the Christ of God: "Ye who sometimes were far off" — all believers of all nations — with those who "are made nigh" — the Jewish Christians. Jesus, our Savior, is "our peace"; by dying on the cross, He completed this miraculous work of making "both one." Gold clasps in blue loops are the symbolical means to this unification. There are divine bands that give strength to this indissoluble unity.

The total number of curtains is ten, indicating our responsibility. They are 28 cubits long (four times seven). This brings to our minds that the God-desired perfection of this mystery applies to the whole earth. Is it not our holy duty to present this perfection visibly?

These ten curtains could also have been sewn together end to end. The length of this band would then be 280 cubits. Remarkably, this corresponds exactly to the length of the white-byssus hanging of the courtyard. The agreement between these two lengths points to the fact that the two coverings represent the church — in the byssus hanging in her outward testimony to the world, but here in the picture of the cherubim covering, she is represented in her glorious worth in union with the beloved Son of the Father. In the counsels of His heart, they are "perfectly joined together." This expression appears *ten* times in the Bible! With the same words, Paul, in three letters, exhorts the assembly of Christ to remember their calling (1 Corinthians 1:10; Ephesians 4:16; Colossians 2:19).

As with the covering of goats' hair, here also there are fifty clasps. Again, this stresses the special importance of this thought: "knit together in love" — the Risen One desires to so see His saints (Colossians 2:2). Could anything else satisfy or glorify Him?

This truth is to a great extent lost to Christendom. The assembly of God is one whole, an indivisible unity. The two groups, believing Jews and believers out of the nations (Gentiles), are inseparably united together by the Holy Spirit who was sent from heaven. "For by one Spirit are we all baptized into one body" (1 Corinthians 12:13).

The blue loops and golden clasps are intended to illustrate to us what "joining" means. "For as the body is one, and hath many members, and all the members of that one body, being many, are one body: so also is Christ" (1 Corinthians 12:12). It is only this unity that corresponds to His purpose and His holy will.

In the obedience of love, shall we not avoid and give up all things that run contrary to the truth? Anything that opposes this unity is sin and grieves the Holy Spirit.

THE ENTRANCE TO THE TABERNACLE

Like the entrance to the courtyard, the entrance to the tabernacle was also on the east side. Five pillars supported the curtain of the entrance through which the

priests had access to the front part of the tabernacle. Here the priestly race was allowed to approach God day and night for ministry. In this place they stood before the face of the Most High to carry out in His holy presence the functions that were ordained of God (Psalm 134:1).

The Spirit of God calls the priestly race of the New Testament "the church of the living God" (1 Timothy 3:15). He speaks of them as people who "were sometime alienated and enemies in [their] mind by wicked works" (Colossians 1:21); "ye were without Christ, . . . having no hope, and without God in the world: but now in Christ Jesus . . . are made nigh by the blood of Christ" (Ephesians 2:12,13). They have the privilege of the "boldness and access with confidence by the faith of him" (Ephesians 3:12)

This house had only one entrance, just as the courtyard had. This one entrance is a type of the Anointed One of

The entrance gate to the dwelling place of God. The curtain of the gate hung on five pillars. It was done in embroidery work and shows the same four colors as the curtain of the gate of the courtyard.

God. In the case of the courtyard the picture pointed more to His humility as Savior of the world; here we see rather the "son over his own house" (Hebrews 3:6). The Lord and Master is seen here in His resurrection glory, crowned with glory and honor. Even the height of ten cubits points to this association. The glorified Christ stands before us.

Now let us turn our attention to the tabernacle itself, which consists of two parts. The front part — two-thirds of the whole — was called "the holy place," the rear third, "the holy of holies." The veil that separated the two rooms was fastened to four pillars.

The Entrance Curtain

It is expected of all true believers as "partakers of the heavenly calling" (Hebrews 3:1) that they "grow in grace, and in the knowledge of our Lord and Saviour Jesus Christ" (2 Peter 3:18). The Holy Spirit desires to spur us on and to instruct us in this. For this purpose, He uses specific portions of the Holy Scriptures, which were transmitted to us by "holy men of God . . . moved by the Holy Ghost" (2 Peter 1:21). What God has given us in the Bible is often insufficiently understood and valued by Christians.

This entrance curtain too is a picture of the Lord Jesus Christ. It is intended to show us something entirely new in addition to the already-described glorious attributes of Jesus Christ. The Lord once said to the eleven disciples: "I have yet many things to say unto you, but ye cannot bear them now. Howbeit when he, the Spirit of truth, is come, he will guide you into all truth" (John 16:12,13).

This expression and promise of the Lord Jesus calls for

our special attention. It tells us that "the whole truth" is yet not to be found in the Gospels. For this to be revealed required the sending of the Advocate. Only after Pentecost and through the weighty writings of the apostles, the full scope of the whole truth about the Lord Jesus Christ and His church was communicated to believers. Paul could therefore solemnly testify to the elders of Ephesus: "I am pure from the blood of all men. For I have not shunned to declare unto you all the counsel of God" (Acts 20:26,27). This true servant of God wrote something of immense importance in his Epistle to the Colossians and thus also to all of us. In accordance with the dispensation of God to him, Paul was "to fulfill the word of God," that is, to bring it to its full measure (Colossians 1:25). These letters are therefore binding and indispensable for our life of faith. We should have the fullest regard for these Epistles, as for all Scripture. Paul emphasizes, "If any man think himself to be a prophet, or spiritual, let him acknowledge that the things that I write unto you are the *commandments of the Lord*" (1 Corinthians 14:37). He could testify to the believing Thessalonians that they did not receive his gospel "as the word of men, but as it is in truth, the Word of God, which effectually worketh also in you that believe" (1 Thessalonians 2:13).

The four familiar colors appear again in the curtain of the entrance to the tabernacle. They emphasize to us the glory of the Risen One, the "son of his love" (Colossians 1:13 ASV). The purple depicts the Crowned One, on whose "head are many diadems" (Revelation 19:12 ASV), while the scarlet recalls the meaningful words "a Lamb as it had been slain" (Revelation 5:6). Lastly, the white byssus gives us to understand that the "Son of man" will come again to judge the world (Daniel 7:13). The Bible applies the title "Son of man" to the Lord Jesus ninety times.

THE FIVE PILLARS OF THE ENTRANCE TO THE TABERNACLE

In these five pillars, which held up the curtain of the gate, we may see a reference to Peter, John, James, Jude, and Paul. In Galatians 2:9 the Holy Spirit describes certain men as "pillars." In their life of faith the writers of the New Testament Epistles reveal themselves as true overcomers. Is not this promise of Jesus Christ for them: "Him that overcometh will I make a pillar in the temple of my God" (Revelation 3:12)?

The Material of the Pillars

The posts of the pillars were made of acacia wood. This wood points to the fact that these men of God possessed the life of Christ. They had become new men through the new birth. The words of Galatians 2:20 had become true of them, as of all true believers: "Christ liveth in me." This wonderful fact produces a deep joy in the heart of every genuine Christian. Paul once asked the Corinthians very solemnly: "Know ye not your own selves, how that Jesus Christ is in you?" (1 Corinthians 13:5).

All the pillars were overlaid with a costly covering. Here we encounter a metal that was not used anywhere in the courtyard: gold, the most valuable of all the metals named in the Bible. It is the appropriate material to depict the righteousness and glory of God. The above-named five servants of the Lord were also clothed with the righteousness of God. They could all appropriate for themselves the great truth: Christ became "righteousness to

The five pillars of the entrance were made of acacia wood covered with gold. Standing on brass bases, they were topped with capitals of gold.

every one that believeth" (Romans 10:4). After his conversion, the one-time Pharisee, Saul of Tarsus, was able to declare freely, "I count all things but loss for the excellency of the knowledge of Christ Jesus my Lord: for whom I have suffered the loss of all things, and do count them but dung . . . not having mine own righteousness, which is of the law, but that which is through the faith of Christ, the *righteousness which is of God* by faith" (Philippians 3:8–9).

The bases of the pillars were of brass. These servants of God were also tested and suffering ones, some of them even martyrs for Jesus' sake. As such, they attained "the crown of righteousness" (2 Timothy 4:8) or the "crown of life" (James 1:12). That is why the pillars were decorated with capitals of gold. These faithful witnesses will not lose their reward. They will one day stand before the judgment seat of Christ wearing their crowns.

The Position of the Pillars

The position of the pillars is of great importance. It is interesting to notice that it is first mentioned after the description of the curtain. Therefore, we may conclude that the entrance curtain and not the pillars had the preeminence. As seen from the Holy of Holies in the tabernacle, the curtain to the entrance concealed the five pillars that held it up. There is an important teaching in this for every servant of God. The Lord Jesus Christ must be seen in our service. He must "have the preeminence" in all things (Colossians 1:18). "My glory will I not give to another," declared the Almighty by the mouth of a prophet (Isaiah 42:8). Paul once said of himself and his co-workers: "For we preach not ourselves, but Christ

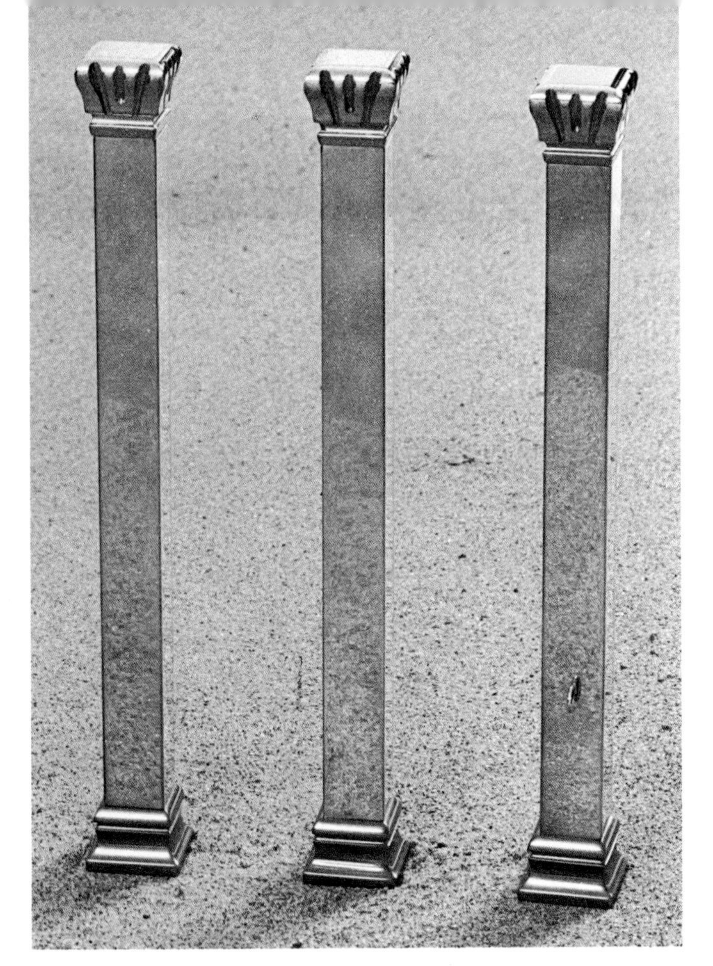

Jesus the Lord; and ourselves your servants for Jesus' sake" (2 Corinthians 4:5). In this, Paul is an impressive example for all servants of Jesus Christ. The five pillars stand *behind* the curtain and stimulate us to earnest self-testing, by which our ministry may be evaluated. If we do not want to become disqualified (1 Corinthians 9:27), this self-judgment is indispensable.

THE GOLDEN WALLS OF THE TABERNACLE

"For ye are the temple of the living God; as God hath said, I will dwell in them . . . and I will be their God, and they shall be my people" (2 Corinthians 6:16). The structure of the tabernacle clearly illustrates this wonderful fact. God's dwelling, His temple, must be built worthy of Him and thus according to His plan.

The curtain of the entrance was ten cubits high. The whole construction was of the same height. The outer form was determined by the width of the boards — each was one and a half cubits wide — and by the number of

the boards of the long side. There was a total of twenty boards, making a length of thirty cubits for the sides. The west wall consisted of eight boards, giving an overall outer measurement of twelve cubits. Since the boards were one cubit thick, the inner breadth was ten cubits. This exactly matches the curtain of the entrance. The front two-thirds of the building had the following inside measurements: a length of twenty cubits and a width of ten cubits. The rear one-third was cube-shaped, each dimension being ten cubits.

THE BOARDS OF THE DWELLING PLACE

The boards of acacia wood formed the important elements of which the tabernacle was constructed. They were covered with gold, and every board stood in two

The walls of the golden house, the dwelling place of the Most High, were made up of twenty boards each on the south and north sides. Eight boards constituted the west wall. All this was in accordance with the plans of God. The front part — called the Holy Place — was twice as long as the Holy of Holies.

heavy sockets of silver, each weighing one talent. Thus each board rested on a base of 120 kilograms (264 lbs.) of silver. The boards of each wall were connected on the outside by four bars or poles, which ran through golden rings. These poles were likewise of acacia wood and covered with gold. A fifth bar that connected the boards of the wall was invisible because it was inserted through a hole drilled horizontally through the middle of the boards.

God had ordered this type of construction in His wisdom. Are we aware of what God wants to bring before us with this? Here, as throughout the building, we behold the miraculous work of the grace of God: He takes men who have been changed through Jesus to build His "spiritual house" upon this earth (1 Peter 2:5).

In the acacia wood, we again see the Lord Jesus Christ, who "is our life" (Colossians 3:4). The boards may be thought to represent all the people who have received life from God by the new birth. This assurance of new life is valuable and is attested by God's Word in 1 John 5:11–13. All believers possess this life, which cannot be lost, cannot die, and is victorious. The love of God gave us the Son, and He gives us this wonderful gift, eternal life. "That whosoever believeth in Him should not perish, but have everlasting life" (John 3:16). "And this is life eternal, that they might know thee the only true God, and Jesus Christ, whom thou hast sent" (John 17:3). "And I give unto them eternal life; and they shall never perish" (John 10:28).

Christ in us! Forty-four times the Holy Scripture speaks of eternal life, seventeen times in John's Gospel alone.

Each of the thick boards or planks of acacia wood covered with gold stood on two bases of silver. The four rings of gold were for the outer poles. The fifth pole ran through the middle of the boards, invisible from the outside.

That is not enough. Every pardoned one is adorned with the beauty of Jesus and clothed with the righteousness of Christ. This is depicted by the covering of gold. So precious ones in the eyes of God are those who are born again that John says of them: "As he is, so are we in this world" (1 John 4:17). We are hardly able to grasp what it means: "Christ Jesus, who of God is made unto us wisdom and righteousness" (1 Corinthians 1:30). We can step into the presence of God only because we are clothed in the righteousness of Jesus Christ.

These boards are a portrait for us for two splendid, incomparable truths that God teaches us: acacia wood means *Christ in us!* "Christ lives in me" (Galatians 2:20). "That Christ may dwell in your hearts by faith" (Ephesians 3:17). The acacia wood with its golden overlay means *We in Christ!* "Therefore if any man be in Christ, he is a new creature: old things are passed away; behold, all things are become new" (2 Corinthians 5:17). "There is therefore now no condemnation to them which are in Christ Jesus" (Romans 8:1).

The silver bases came from the ransom money of the numbered Israelites (Exodus 30:11–16). This ransom money totaled one hundred talents. It was melted down and molded into the bases or sockets for the boards (Exodus 38:25–27). The 1,775 shekels of silver referred to in Exodus 38:25–28 — and which were additional to the 100 talents — were used for making the hooks and capitals of the pillars, and also the fillets. With great wonder we read what God's spokesman, Job's friend, proclaimed at that time: God will be merciful to men. He speaks to the one sent of the Lord: "Deliver him from going down to the pit; I have found a ransom" (Job 33:24; cf. 1 John 4:10).

We know this One sent of God. He is Jesus Christ. He is the ransom for our eternal salvation. This expression appears fourteen times in the Bible. The son of God designates Himself as the ransom (Matthew 20:28). How costly was our purchase (1 Corinthians 6:20)! Does He have all our love?

There were two bases for each board. A twofold salvation was obtained for us: the salvation of the soul (Hebrews 10:39) and the salvation of the body (Romans 8:11,23). Both are of infinite worth. The one is even now a wonderful fact; the other will become a reality in indescribable glory, when mortality is swallowed up by the immortal life (2 Corinthians 5:4).

Paul described both processes with the words "Christ . . . hath abolished death, and hath brought life and immortality to light through the gospel" (2 Timothy 1:10). Such a foundation was prepared according to God's plan for each board and is given to every child of God. It is the "grace wherein we stand" (Romans 5:2). "By faith ye stand" (2 Corinthians 1:24).

These bases of silver separated the acacia wood from the sandy soil. So also the saved, the redeemed, are surely in the world, but no longer of the world. Our Lord Jesus Christ "gave himself for our sins, that he might deliver us

Here we see the west wall. The four poles of acacia wood were covered with gold. They connected the boards of the walls on the outside and formed them into a unit.

from this present evil world, according to the will of God and our Father: to whom be glory for ever and ever. Amen" (Galatians 1:4–5).

THE POLES

The poles were solely for holding together the boards that formed the walls of the dwelling. They were fashioned from acacia wood and covered with gold. They rested in golden rings fastened to the boards. The materials of the poles — acacia wood and gold — lead us to conclude that, like the boards, they have a typical meaning. They are a picture of believers, who, living according to the command of the Lord Jesus Christ, are called upon to provide the needed strength for the entire structure. In the Epistle to the Ephesians Paul pictures men of God whose responsibility it was to serve the church for spiritual benefit. We can here distinguish four groups of pardoned people, whom the resurrected Christ, in His holy care and concern, appointed for His assembly.

"And He gave some, *apostles;* and some, *prophets;* and some, *evangelists;* and some, *pastors* and *teachers;* for the perfecting of the saints, for the work of the ministry, for the edifying of the body of Christ." Thus, the goal and purpose of God was, first, the unity of the faith and the knowledge of the Son of God, and second, full growth in Him who is the Head. The whole body "fitly joined together and compacted by that which every joint supplieth" (Ephesians 4:9–16).

How beautifully these words describe the work and purpose of the four outer poles in their New Testament significance. These gifts of Christ are of inestimable

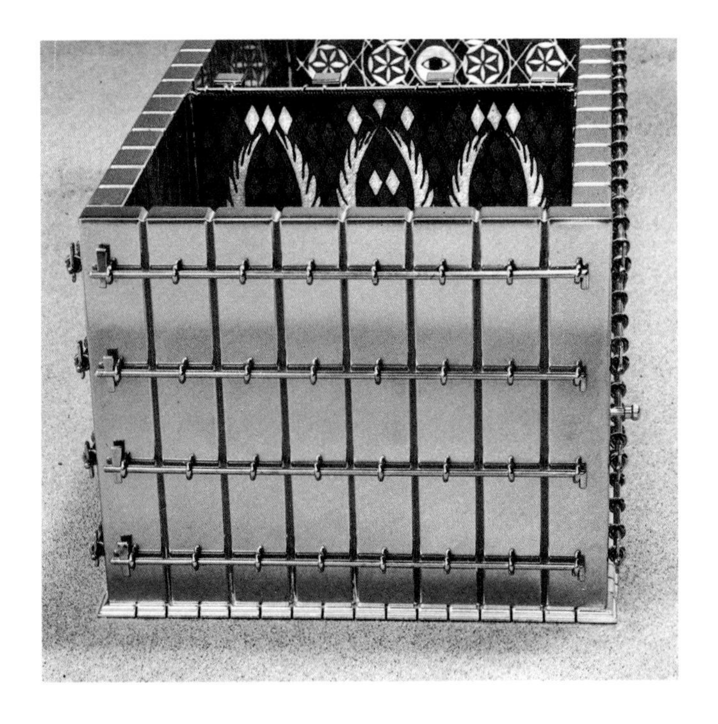

worth for the stability and prosperity of the church. They form an organic part of the whole.

Even though the apostles and prophets are no longer personally present among us, their blessed ministry still benefits us today to a great extent. Their writings, inspired by the Holy Spirit and preserved by the grace of God, enable us to partake of the fruit of their labor to our lasting benefit. For the rest, we rejoice in the ministry of the evangelist, the pastor, and the teacher. We should be thankful for this ministry and in humility and love recognize and support those who exercise it. The ministry of these gifts can never be administered on an organizational basis. No human authority can equip and appoint men to it. That is an exclusive right of the risen Lord, the Head of the assembly.

The poles fulfilled their purpose in that, placed through *the golden rings,* they held the whole building together. How emphatically these details remind us of an important fact in accordance with the desire of God: The ministry with the above-named gifts is a ministry of love; for this reason the rings were of gold. Only godly love may be the true motive for the exercise of the ministry: "And if I have the gift of prophecy, and know all mysteries and all knowledge . . . but have not love, I am nothing" (1 Corinthians 13:2 ASV; cf. Ephesians 4:16). The Holy Spirit mentions these rings thirty-five times (five times seven). Does He not desire to illustrate by this the value and significance of this love, "which is the bond of perfectness" (Colossians 3:14)?

One pole remained almost invisible. It ran horizontally through the middle of the boards and served to bind them from within. That reminds us of this wonderful expression: *"Christ in you,* the hope of glory" (Colossians 1:27).

Only when the poles were inserted in their places did the whole structure have the stability God wished it to have.

The love of the Lord works within us all today to make the obedience of faith not only a confession of the lips, but a necessity for life. Our behavior demonstrates whether this "joining together" is a serious matter for us. We do not want, nor are we able, to be satisfied with a spiritual unity without a visible expression of that unity. It is our holy duty to refrain from and shun all that which violates the loving will of our Master. The beloved Son implored the Father concerning us: ". . . that they *all may be one* . . . that the world may believe that thou has sent me" (John 17:21). The fulfillment of the request of our Lord certainly includes a *visible* unity of the children of God.

It is striking that the Holy Spirit declares *five times* in the letters of the apostle Paul that the children of God are to be fully and blessedly united (1 Corinthians 1:10; 12:24; Ephesians 2:21; 4:16; Colossians 2:19).

4. The Holy Place

THE INTERIOR OF THE TABERNACLE

The Holy Spirit laid upon the heart of David and upon his lips what should fill every one of us as we enter the sanctuary. Only holy motives can cause one filled with the spirit of a priest to dwell there where the Lord has promised His most holy presence: "One thing have I asked of Jehovah, that will I seek after: that I may dwell in the house of Jehovah all the days of my life, to behold the beauty of Jehovah, and to inquire in his temple" (Psalm 27:4 ASV).

"So have I looked upon thee in the sanctuary, to see thy power and thy glory" (Psalm 63:2 ASV).

The priests were allowed to enter this place only with bare feet — they wore no sandals (cf. Exodus 3:5). The table of shewbread stood on the north side of the tabernacle, the candlestick on the south side opposite it, and on the west side directly before the veil was the altar of incense.

If we picture this arrangement of the most holy vessels as a line that runs from the brazen altar to the altar of incense, with another imaginary line running from the golden table across the tabernacle to the candlestick, we perceive a cross!

Only on the basis of the precious Offering on the cross can a person enter into the tabernacle of God. And here the knowledge of Jesus Christ is wonderfully expanded and deepened. For the first time since Calvary, there is a priestly race that is called and sanctified not by natural descent, from Aaron, but by divine grace. Those who form this priesthood today may experience blessed fellowship with God the Father and partake of the joy of His heart in the Son of His love. The priests of God can cry aloud, "We have thought of thy lovingkindness, O God, in the midst of thy temple. According to thy name, O God, so is thy praise unto the ends of the earth" (Psalm 48:9–10). "And in his temple doth every one speak of his glory" (Psalm 29:9).

When the saints and beloved of the Lord Jesus gather together in His name, they are the visible expression of the "habitation of God through the Spirit" (Ephesians 2:22). This gives them a special opportunity to practice their priestly ministry.

However, it is an indispensable prerequisite for this ministry, that even at home in daily living they lead a spiritual life and manifest a priestly attitude of mind. Only then can they worship "in spirit and in truth" (John 4:24; cf. 1 Peter 2:5).

What conclusion can we draw? What does all this mean?

Every sin in the life of a believer, such as complacency, lukewarmness, and conformity to the world, grieves the Holy Spirit. Sins must be confessed to God, condemned, and judged by the guilty one. Then He in His grace forgives, cleanses, and gives new peace (1 John 1:9). Now the Spirit of God can fill the heart afresh.

Yes, and even more: it is the Holy Spirit's desire that the believer grow inwardly and be continually blessed with renewed joy by earnest study of the Word of God and through intimate fellowship with the Lord Jesus. The more he grows in grace and knowledge of his Lord and Savior, the more he desires to testify of this fullness of blessing before his God and Father.

The "man of God" (1 Timothy 6:11), then, is like the Israelite in Deuteronomy 26. This man came with his basket full of the firstfruits to the house of God "the place which Jehovah thy God shall choose, to cause his name to dwell there" (Deuteronomy 26:2 ASV). There is the place where God desires to be worshiped. Twenty-one times the Holy Spirit, therefore, emphasizes in Deuteronomy 12–31 this place as the dwelling place of God. Only there can the offerer praise the Giver in the God-ordained manner for the earthly blessings and present Him with gifts he has brought as a thank offering.

So also today the believer goes with a happy heart to the sanctuary, the church. It is his desire to render homage in worship to the Father for the spiritual blessings he has received.

Through the grace of God he has recognized these blessings and has made them his own by faith. He is totally filled by Jesus Christ. God's "unspeakable gift" makes him profoundly happy (2 Corinthians 9:15).

THE TABLE OF SHEWBREAD

The table of shewbread is a picture of Jesus Christ, who in His grace guarantees the security of His own. It is called "the pure table" and is mentioned twenty-one times by

Moses (Leviticus 24:6). The number twenty-one speaks for itself, three times seven meaning divine perfection.

The table of shewbread was made of *acacia wood* and covered with pure gold. Here we first meet this most valuable metal: *pure gold.* So we can recognize in this picture our Lord Jesus in His true *humanity* and, at the same time, in His true godhead. Gold — in all the utensils and furnishings we have considered up to this point — represented divine righteousness and glory. Now, "pure gold" speaks of deity itself.

The height of the golden table was one and a half cubits — the same height as the grate of the brazen altar. On the altar lay the wood and the sacrifice and on the table lay the fruit of the offering: the shewbread made from the fine flour of the wheat.

Around the edge of the table ran two vertical borders of pure gold. They were arranged one on top of the other.

Inside the tabernacle on the north side stood the table of shewbread. Opposite it was the candlestick; before the Holy of Holies was the incense altar. To the west hung the veil with the cherubim forms supported by the four pillars.

The lower border, "a handbreadth round about," kept the shewbread from falling from the table. This detail causes us to think with joy of what the Lord has promised: "Neither shall any man pluck them out of my hand" (John 10:28). The upper border is a wreath or crown — a decoration we see here for the first time. This is of great significance, for it shows us the Lord Jesus, who was crowned with glory and honor by the Father after His completed work of salvation (Hebrews 2:9). No longer the crown of thorns, but the victor's crown now adorns His head!

Attached to the table of shewbread were also two carrying staves, which rested in golden rings; they were made of acacia wood covered with pure gold. The Lord Jesus Christ has a special honor and glory since His resurrection: He is our *Shepherd* as well as the *Overseer* of our souls (1 Peter 2:25 ASV).

As the Good Shepherd, Jesus laid down His life for the sheep (John 10:11). But as the "great shepherd, " He is for all the redeemed the guarantor of their preservation, nurture, and care (Psalm 23; Hebrews 13:20–21) and carries them as the golden table carried the shewbread. His love is solicitously attentive to the welfare of His saints. The golden rings, in which lay the carrying staves, are a picture of His love. His mighty hands and His powerful love care for all whom the Father has given Him as the fruit of the travail of His soul. These whom He so loves in truth have a mighty Lord who faithfully cares for them!

THE SHEWBREAD

The shewbread was made of fine flour. Two-tenths of an ephah was required for every loaf, which amounted to about 4.5 liters. The fine flour is above all a beautiful, appropriate picture for the pure and spotless humanity of our Lord Jesus. It corresponds to some extent to the costly byssus cloth — fine and pure. Fine flour has no coarse elements. The life of Jesus shows — corresponding to this figure — complete agreement between grace and truth, and that in a perfection in which the heart of God deeply rejoiced.

The kernel of wheat that falls into the earth and dies produces much fruit. The harvested sheaves must be threshed by hard blows, and the kernels must be ground between hard millstones to make the flour. The fine flour, made into dough, must first endure the heat of the oven to become edible bread. How striking and impressive are these steps necessary for the making of bread. They all testify to the unconditional devotion of the One who went to death to the eternal glory of God.

"O Father! One is there above all others and Thou dost look upon Him with pleasure, Thine own beloved Son. As in eternity, so He was in the fullness of time, and now sits as Man upon Thy throne." So sing the children of God who join with the Father in rejoicing in the Son of His love.

The incense in the golden bowls upon the layers of bread completes this wonderful picture: the Lord Jesus Christ is the pleasant, fragrant aroma for the heart of God.

The shewbread lay for seven days before the presence of God, to be replaced by new bread every Sabbath. The old bread served as food for the priests. It was eaten in a holy place. That was not, however, in the tabernacle itself, but in the courtyard next to the brazen altar (Leviticus 10:12–13). When the priests ate the shewbread, they gave expression to fellowship with God by that act. Manna was the food of the people of God in the wilderness, but nourishment for the priests was supplied by these loaves. It was a special privilege for the ministers of the Lord.

The Lord Jesus Christ is "the bread of life" for all those of a priestly mind. It is this that these loaves of shewbread depict. As a most holy item of the offerings made by fire unto the Lord, they could be eaten only by those who lived and served in this holy place (Leviticus 24:9).

How are we spiritually nourished? Do we belong to this class of people?

There were twelve loaves. They lay in two layers on the pure table and so direct our attention to the tribes of Israel as a total people — undivided, as God had always beheld them.

In spite of Israel's centuries-long exile, Paul constantly held to this thought. As he spoke before king Agrippa, he spoke of Israel as "our twelve tribes" (Acts 26:6–7). One day, in the messianic kingdom, the full number of tribes will again be present to the praise of the grace of God. So testified the prophet Ezekiel (37:16–22).

We encounter the number twelve often; Jesus, for example, had twelve disciples.

These loaves of shewbread surely also point to the totality of the church of Jesus Christ. She is "the fruit of the travail of his soul" (Isaiah 53:11).

It is striking that the incense was on the bread "for a memorial" (Leviticus 24:7). The incense on the loaves, not the loaves themselves, was burned for God. The Lord Jesus gives His saints value, for they are before God "a

The golden table of shewbread was adorned with a decorative border of a handbreadth and a golden crown. On the table lay two stacks of bread, which were replaced every Sabbath with fresh loaves. Golden bowls full of powdered incense were placed on top of the stacks of bread.

sweet savour of Christ" (2 Corinthians 2:15). God has placed the acceptability of His Son on His saints. They are made well-pleasing to God through it. By this, all believers are reminded of something wonderful: They are forever "accepted in the beloved" (Ephesians 1:6).

The full number of these loaves illustrates for us that *only the unity* of the saved is acceptable to God. This alone, not selfish division, corresponds to His holy decree. The Holy Spirit emphasizes "the unity of the Spirit in the bond of peace" in Ephesians 4:1–4. Does this word exercise power and authority for our conscience? This does not stress the requirement to uniformity and identity of opinion. We are much rather required to be zealous to maintain intact and visible the Holy Spirit — created unity of the body of Christ. Are we ready to repent and to walk in the obedience of faith in a godly manner?

This is what happens when we realize that the essence of the church is much more than the separate organizations that we call "churches," and that this unity of all believers in Christ must also come to wider expression.

The number twelve also symbolizes administration. The Lord entrusted the twelve apostles with authority for the administration of all that He had left with them. Subsequently he extended this task to His whole assembly. This includes admission to participation in the Lord's Supper and to fellowship at the table of the Lord, but it also included exclusion from it (Matthew 18:15–20; John 20:22–23; 1 Corinthians 4:1–2, 5:9–13).

When the dwelling place of God was erected, it is related of Moses: "And he put the table in the tent of the congregation . . . and he set the bread *in order*" (Exodus 40:22,23). That causes us to think of the words "joying

and beholding your order, and the stedfastness of your faith in Christ" (Colossians 2:5). This is a spiritual pattern of behavior fitting to the honor of God: "Let all things be done decently and in order." Here is a clear directive for the gathering of the saints (1 Corinthians 14:40). There should be no stiff formality of deadening legalism in the church, but rather a doing of good, a spiritual leadership, and an orderliness exercised in love. "That thou mayest know how thou oughtest to behave thyself in the house of God, which is the church of the living God" (1 Timothy 3:15), where all, both young and old, are responsible, but are also led. For "where no wise guidance is, the people falleth" (Proverbs 11:14 ASV).

Here we gladly hold fast the instruction of Romans 12:4–8. To the shame of many Christians, these words remain largely neglected. They serve our best interest, however, when they determine our actions: "For as we have many members in one body, and all members have not the same office: so we, being many, are one body in Christ . . . having then gifts differing according to the grace that is given to us, whether prophecy, let us prophesy according to the proportion of faith; or ministry, let us wait on our ministering: or he that teacheth, on teaching;

or he that exhorteth, on exhortation; he that giveth, let him do it with simplicity; he that ruleth, with diligence; he that sheweth mercy, with cheerfulness."

What a diversity all this shows of the gifts of grace in the assembly of God! In the ministry of love, all the members of the body of Christ are allowed to come to full maturity. This will cause the assembly to prosper and be at peace where the Lord has ordained blessing and life forever (Psalm 133:3).

THE PURE CANDLESTICK

"The Lord said that he would dwell in the thick darkness." Solomon made known this decree to the people of God, as the holy God occupied His throne in His temple in Jerusalem (1 Kings 8:12). This expression of the Spirit-filled king facilitates the understanding of the meaning of the golden candlestick.

"God is light," He Himself. Therefore He has no need of natural light, even less of artificial light. Now we understand why there were no windows in the tabernacle. It had to be so. The living God revealed Himself there.

The full revelation of God is the Man Christ Jesus. Twenty-one times, therefore, the Son of God is called "the light" in the Gospels. This is significant, for three times seven is the godly number of perfection.

In the Book of Revelation John describes for us the heavenly Jerusalem at the time of the end: "And the city had no need of the sun, neither of the moon, to shine in it: for the *glory of God* did lighten it, and the Lamb is the light thereof" (Revelation 21:23). The candlestick of pure gold witnesses here also to God in His incomparable glory.

The material for the preparation of the candlestick was one talent, which corresponds to 60 kilograms (132 lbs.) of pure gold. Therefore it is called "the pure candlestick" (Leviticus 24:1–4). The Word of God speaks of this most holy vessel thirty times, but gives no dimensions for it; certainly it is for the reason that the glory of Jesus Christ is immeasurable. It is the principal task of the Holy Spirit to continually direct our attention to the glory of the risen and elevated Christ.

The product was finished in "beaten work." By contrast, the golden calf of Aaron was only molten, a miserable product of human imagination (Exodus 32:4). To form the candlestick, the craftsmen had to make innumerable hammer blows. This causes us quite naturally to think of the words "that Christ should suffer" and that He "should be the first that should rise from the dead, and should *shew* light" (Acts 26:23).

Jesus, the Risen One, brought the full light of the revelation of God to us. How powerfully the account concerning the Lord Jesus in Romans 1:4 speaks to us: "And declared to be the Son of God with power, according to the spirit of holiness, by the resurrection from the dead." May God's grace illuminate our hearts more and more with the "light of the knowledge of the glory of God in the face of Jesus Christ" (2 Corinthians 4:6)!

The *seven* lamps filled with oil, which were attached to the upper end of the candlestick and its six branches, are a witness to perfect light. This fullness of light is described in the prophecy concerning the Messiah of Israel in Isaiah 11:2: "And the spirit of the Lord shall rest upon him, the spirit of wisdom and understanding, the spirit of counsel and might, the spirit of knowledge and of the fear of the

Lord." The Lord Jesus Christ was filled with the Spirit of God in a unique manner.

We are struck by the fact that the Messiah in this Scripture text is named "the branch" and the fruit-bearing "shoot," a plant that God had planted. Therefore the candlestick had to be decorated with twenty-two blossom cups, "knop and flower." These were opened almond blossoms with five petals each. If we are to understand the real significance of this detail, we must look at a verse in the prophecy of Jeremiah.

Jeremiah had a vision at the time of his call to the prophetic ministry. God asked him, "What seest thou?" And he answered, "I see a rod of an almond tree" (Jeremiah 1:11–12). The almond tree begins to bloom before all other trees. With its snow-white blossoms, it proclaims new life when spring begins and the winter death of the plant world comes to an end.

God chose this detail appropriately. The almond blossoms give the candlestick a definite meaning. It is a picture of the Lord Jesus, "who hath abolished death, and hath brought life and immortality to light" (2 Timothy 1:10).

The rod of Aaron also was an almond rod! It lay one night in the Holy of Holies before the ark of the covenant, with the rods of the other eleven princes of Israel. The next morning it alone had shown signs of new life, for it "brought forth buds, and bloomed blossoms, and yielded almonds" (Numbers 17:1–11). Here too it is also clear to us that the fruit-bearing almond rod is a picture of our risen Lord. He is and remains the eternal High Priest of His beloved people.

The twenty-two (two times eleven) almond blossoms of

the candlestick are a supreme testimony to the glory of the One who was awakened from the dead. Two is the known number of witnesses required by God (2 Corinthians 13:1). The number eleven has already been seen in the number of curtains made of goats' hair; it is the number that first exceeds ten and is the measure of responsibility. The twenty-two blossom cups are a powerful testimony from Him and about Him, the Christ of God. He alone has the right to the name "the faithful and true witness" (Revelation 1:5; 3:14).

The six branches of the candlestick were "out of it"; that is, made of one piece, grown together, so to speak, as an integral part of it. The words of Romans 6:5 are familiar to us: "For if we have been planted together in the likeness of His death, we shall be also in the likeness of His resurrection." All this points to a God-given, indissoluble unity. Only when the six branches are a part of the candlestick is it what it should actually be; they are its decoration and its ornamentation. Of the church of Jesus, the body of Jesus Christ, we read: "The fulness of him that filleth all in all" (Ephesians 1:23), His wonderful complement.

Without the lampstand itself, the branches likewise are without importance. It gives them their value and true significance. This unique fact fills us with a holy wonder, and our hearts are touched as we read: "For in him dwelleth all the fulness of the Godhead bodily. And ye are complete in him. . . ." The apostle expects from all who are rooted and grounded in this faith that, full of thanksgiving, they glorify the God of all grace (Colossians 2:7,9–10). It is the continual task of the Holy Spirit to remind us afresh of this truth. Full fellowship with the

Lord Jesus is the secret of the new life. "For both he that sanctifieth and they who are sanctified are all one" (Hebrews 2:11). He is not ashamed to call these saints His "brethren." He can expect them, therefore, to exhibit the fruit of true faith: spiritual energy, growing knowledge, self-control, patience, godliness, brotherly love, and *agape,* the divine love (2 Peter 1:5–7 ASV).

The candlestick with its six branches teaches us that the Lord Jesus Christ is our life and our light. "To you who believe He is precious." Everything was given to us in and through Him. Just as Eve was taken from the side of Adam and was one with him, so the church comes out of the risen Christ and remains one with Him. A wonderful secret!

"Knobs and blossoms" of the candlestick draw our attention to the fact that here also fruit is expected. Everything is from Him: life and fruit. The organic connection with the Lord Jesus Christ produces fruit spontaneously. We are members of "him who is raised from the dead, that we should bring forth fruit unto God" (Romans 7:4). Let us therefore encourage one another by the prayer wish of the apostle Paul, which applies to us in the same way as to the saints of Philippi: to be filled "with the fruits of righteousness, which are by Jesus Christ, unto the glory and praise of God" (Philippians 1:11).

The shaft of the candlestick was found exactly in the center of the six branches. So also the central place always belongs to the Lord Jesus. He should and must be the central point. Twelve times the Word of God shows us the Lord Jesus Christ "in the center," whether it is on the cross or on the throne. Further, we see Him in the midst of the glorified saints in heaven as they surround Him and worship and praise Him as the Lamb of God (Revelation 5:6).

The prophet Zephaniah sees Him as the central point of His earthly people, of the believing remnant of Israel. In the millennium He will pour out the promised blessing on His people. "The Lord thy God in the midst of thee is mighty; he will save, he will rejoice over thee with joy; he will rest in his love, he will joy over thee with singing" (Zephaniah 3:17). What a heart-moving, uplifting promise of God for His earthly people.

The Lord Jesus occupies the central place in the church also. He is in the center, "that in all things he might have the preeminence" (Colossians 1:18); this is the plan of the Father's love — the purpose of God. He is the One who is chief "among ten thousand" (Song of Solomon 5:10).

The shaft of the candlestick carried more blossoms than each of its arms. This too is a pointer to Jesus. For He will be "fruitful among his brethren" (Hosea 13:15). The believer is filled with indescribable joy as he contemplates the glory of Jesus.

THE LIGHT OF THE CANDLESTICK

The light of the candlestick was fed from the pure oil of the lamps. Every Christian knows that the oil is a picture of the Holy Spirit. The third person of the Godhead was sent to earth after the glorious resurrection of the Lord Jesus Christ. And where does He now dwell on the earth? God revealed it in His Word: ". . . that he may abide with you forever. . . . he dwelleth with you, and shall be in you" (John 14:16,17); ". . . The Holy Ghost which dwelleth in us" (2 Timothy 1:14). He is the seal, the

The golden candlestick had six branches that were made of one piece with it. The seven bowls on the ends contained the pure oil for the light. Twenty-two almond blossoms, knobs and blossoms, decorated the whole piece, which was hammered out of one talent of pure gold.

anointing and the pledge of all true believers, who belong to the Lord Jesus (2 Corinthians 1:21–22).

The Holy Spirit, "the promise of the Father," is the wonderful gift of the love of God. This is why God calls us to "be filled with the Spirit" (Ephesians 5:18). That is His positive will for us, for only so can we be lights for the Lord and shine like the lights of heaven in a dark world (Philippians 2:15).

The candlestick was not placed just anywhere, say, in the courtyard, or even outside of this holy area. Its place could be only in the tabernacle. There its lights shone and illuminated the room. It was positioned near the south wall, opposite the table of shewbread. That the candlestick had its place in the tabernacle points to the fact that the Holy Spirit is given only to the true church. He lives only in the assembly of God. The world can no more receive Him than those who are only nominal believers. Our Lord made this completely clear in John 14:17.

The light of the lamps fell first on the candlestick itself. This shows us what is the most exalted task and joy of the Holy Spirit: "He shall glorify me," said the Lord Jesus (John 16:14). This is also the first and foremost task for all His Spirit-filled witnesses. Are you one of them?

The light of the lamps shone in the tabernacle. This shows us that there is no church of Jesus Christ apart from the Holy Spirit. Through the Holy Spirit the living God gives to His assembly the fullness of His light. But the thoughts of God from His Word can be shown by His wonderful light only when the Spirit of the Lord is not grieved by unfaithfulness, selfish service to God, and human precepts. Let us therefore be among those who deeply honor and obey the directions of the Lord Jesus

Christ, above all those that concern His presence in the midst of His blood-bought church. He, in His faithfulness, will then illuminate us with His light. "Light is sown for the righteous, and gladness for the upright in heart" (Psalm 97:11). "Unto the upright there ariseth light in the darkness" (Psalm 112:4).

The rays of light from the candlestick fell on the golden incense altar and on the golden table with the shewbread, which are a picture of the unity of the people of God. The rays of light from the candlestick fell also on the golden walls, of which the tabernacle was constructed. The walls draw our attention to the complete unity that is a characteristic of the church of God. This abundance of light also illuminated the colors of the cherubim covering, which we have seen as a revelation of the glory of Jesus Christ and His church. It also illuminated the hangings of the dwelling place of the Most High, which were connected with golden clasps. So here the Spirit-wrought and God-desired unity of the body of Jesus Christ is brought before us.

Are we walking in the light of this truth and do we allow ourselves to be regulated by it? If so, we conform to the priestly dignity and calling of the children of God. The priests were illuminated by this light as they performed their ministry at the golden altar. Only so could they fulfill the requirements prescribed by God and stand before the presence of the Most High.

THE VESSELS OF THE TABERNACLE

The snuffers and the tongs were used in the care of the lamps. They also were of pure gold (Exodus 25:38; 1 Kings 7:50). What tasks was the high priest to perform with these vessels?

Every evening and every morning Aaron performed a holy ministry that consisted of cleaning and lighting the lamps (Exodus 27:20–21). Each lamp wick was consumed by use. Its flame flickered and smoked and the wick carbonized. The priest was to prevent this. He first of all extinguished the flickering light by means of the snuffer. Then he took the sooty wick of the lamp and shortened it with the trimmers, so that the light could burn brightly and steadily again (Leviticus 24:1–4).

To see to it that the light of the candlestick would shine "from evening until morning" was the responsibility given to Aaron himself to perform with diligent care, for a continual light was to burn before the presence of God (Exodus 30:7–8; Numbers 8:2–3).

This continual light brought out the beauty of *the candlestick* in a unique manner. In this it is an important type for us. The Holy Spirit is grieved when Christians consider themselves to be of great importance and place themselves in a prominent position. The true servant of the Lord will say with the psalmist: "Not unto us, O Jehovah, not unto us, but unto thy name give glory, for thy lovingkindness and for thy truth's sake. . . . But we will bless Jehovah from this time forth and for evermore. Praise ye Jehovah" (Psalm 115:1,18 ASV).

If we appropriate the honor of our Lord, whether in a flagrant or more subtle manner, the light of our lamp is darkened and it begins to flicker. The wicks are then full of soot; they have become unusable. The Lord, as the Servant of His tabernacle, must then use the snuffer and trimmer on us. It may be shaming and painful, but His action serves for our cleansing and correction. When He has finished His work in us, we can serve Him again as "children of light" (Ephesians 5:8).

In this is fulfilled the wish of all the righteous: "The light of the righteous rejoiceth" (Proverbs 13:9).

"And he made the vessels which were upon the table, his dishes, and his spoons, and his bowls, and his covers to cover withal, of pure gold" (Exodus 37:16).

The preparations for the priestly offices called for the oil pitcher, the mortar and pestle, and the mixing bowls for the holy anointing oil.

As we consider these vessels, we are naturally reminded of the words of 2 Timothy 2:20–21, where the Christian's attention is drawn to a matter of special import. He should be a vessel that is cleansed and separated from the dishonorable vessels. Only so can he be sanctified and therefore useful, serviceable, and prepared for every good work for the Master. This desire of the Master of the house spurs the earnest believer on to conform to this picture in his actions and his thinking. He most earnestly desires to be used by his Lord to His honor.

The necessary conditions for being used by the Lord may not be taken lightly or overlooked. Often they demand earnest and sometimes even painful changes within the people of God: "Abstain from all appearance [or 'every form'] of evil" (1 Thessalonians 5:22). This can even mean that one must separate himself, according to the will of God, from those who willfully hold fast to traditions that are contrary to God and who tolerate both corrupt teachings and sinful conduct.

The Drink-Offering Pitcher

The drink-offering pitcher (Exodus 29:38–40) contained wine, which was not drunk but offered. The wine was a prescribed part of the continual burnt offerings, and was never to be omitted.

The Bible mentions the drink offering sixty-four times. These offerings were brought to the living God as a sacrifice on the altar in the courtyard of the tabernacle. Their importance will be well understood with the help of Psalm 104:15. Wine is mentioned there as the picture of earthly, God-given joy that God in His goodness grants to the sons of men.

Our Lord and Savior desired to glorify God. His consecration was thus a service to God and at the same time a renunciation of the joys of this world. His complete joy was to serve His God without reserve. This was the expression of his heart: "And there is none upon earth that I desire beside thee" (Psalm 73:25).

The drink offering was poured out, causing us to think about the words of Isaiah 53:12: "He hath poured out his soul unto death. . . ." The Word of God says of His dedication: "My offering and my bread . . . for a sweet savour unto me" (Exodus 29:40–41; Leviticus 23:13,18; Numbers 28–29).

According to Psalm 16:4, there were idol worshipers who offered their gods a drink offering of blood. Godless Jews spoke presumptuously against Jeremiah. They further declared in arrogant defiance: "We will certainly . . . burn incense to the queen of heaven, and . . . pour out drink offerings unto her" (Jeremiah 44:17). These drink offerings could have consisted of blood, but also of wine. In the heathen cults, it was the practice of the priests to become drunk and prophesy in their stupor. "The priest and the prophet have erred through strong drink, they are swallowed up of wine." The fact that this had to be said also of the priests of the true God brought upon them deserved judgment (Isaiah 28:7).

The sin of the two sons of Aaron, Nadab and Abihu, lies in this that they offered "strange fire." The fire of God consumed these sacrilegious men immediately. What God commanded the priests directly following this judgment appears to stand in direct connection with the tragedy: "Do not drink wine nor strong drink, thou, nor thy sons with thee, when you go into the tabernacle of the congregation, lest ye die." It is entirely possible that the two sons of the priest drank the wine of the drink offering

and became intoxicated with it (Leviticus 10:1–3; 8–9).

"I will be sanctified in them that come nigh me, and before all the people I will be glorified." Thus declares the statement of the Lord. These priests robbed God and took for themselves something that belonged alone to Him. To them was addressed the question: "Will a man rob God?" (Malachi 3:8).

How good it is, in contrast, to read the significant words of the apostle Paul, who had been tested by suffering, in his letter to the Philippians from Rome: "But even if I am being poured out like a drink offering on the sacrifice and service coming from your faith, I am glad and rejoice with all of you. So you too should be glad and rejoice with me" (Philippians 2:17–18 NIV).

The joyful dedication of the Philippians in the battle for the gospel was viewed by God as a living sacrifice (Romans 12:1; 15–16). Paul crowns this offering, so to speak, with his martyrdom. By this he gives a wonderful example of true humility and spiritual attitude. Truly, he lived a dedicated, God-consecrated life (2 Timothy 4:6).

The Mortar and Pestle

The mortar and pestle were used for crushing the olives to obtain pure oil. They also served for securing "pure

For the services of the priests, different vessels were available: mortar and pestle, oil jugs, incense bowls, drink-offering jugs, and mixing bowls for the oil of the anointing and the holy spices.

The incense altar before the Holy of Holies was fashioned from acacia wood and covered with fine gold. A golden wreath decorated the cover with the four horns. The incense container, filled with burning coals from the brazen altar, served for the burning of the incense in the Holy of Holies.

incense" from the sweet-smelling spices, the hardened resin drops and other components were ground to powder (Exodus 30:22–38). Both "the oil of the holy anointing" and the incense were considered most holy. Their components were "crushed."

This causes us to think of the manifold sufferings of the Lord Jesus Christ, which, according to the plan of His God and Father, were necessary for the work of salvation. The incense was intended exclusively for God.

The oil of anointing is a picture of the Holy Spirit, who, on the basis of the atoning sufferings of the Lord Jesus, was poured out upon all believers. Only truly converted people can receive this gift, for the anointing oil was not to be poured "upon man's flesh" (Exodus 30:32; Ephesians 1:12–14).

Paul sees himself bound together to one great unity with all those who are born again when he writes, "Now he which stablisheth us with you in Christ, and hath anointed us, is God; who hath also sealed us, and given the earnest of the Spirit in our hearts" (2 Corinthians 1:21–22). The gift of the Holy Spirit is of definite importance for our life of faith.

On the day that Moses had fully set up the tabernacle (Numbers 7:1), it was anointed and thus sanctified to God. This applied to the dwelling place and all that was inside it, including the brazen altar and the laver (Exodus 40:9–16). Everything had to be in keeping with the holy God who in His grace was about to live here with redeemed men.

The anointing and sanctification of believers through the Spirit of God is indispensable for all that concerns and pertains to our worship and service. Only the gift of the

Holy Spirit and His leading can give us the necessary insight, understanding, and power for service in the presence of God.

This is fully confirmed by the words of the Lord Jesus when He said to the Samaritan woman at the well in Sychar: "But the hour cometh, and now is, when the true worshippers shall worship the Father in spirit and in truth: for the Father seeketh such to worship him. God is a Spirit: and they that worship him must worship him in spirit and in truth" (John 4:23–24).

"But ye have an unction from the Holy One, and ye know all things" (1 John 2:20). This statement is made to all who are rightly designated "a holy priesthood." Their exalted task is "to offer up spiritual sacrifices, acceptable to God by Jesus Christ" (1 Peter 2:5).

THE GOLDEN ALTAR OF INCENSE

It is natural to compare the golden altar of incense with the brazen altar. The brazen altar reminds us of Calvary, where every sinner can find forgiveness and be reconciled to God. On the blood-drenched hill of Calvary, our beloved Lord effected an eternal redemption through His sacrificial death. No one can measure the value and the significance of this once-for-all event. Our hearts are touched anew again and again when we behold the sacrificial death of our Lord and they are filled with deepest thanksgiving and holy joy.

The difference between the two altars lay not in their meanings, but in their location: The brazen altar stood outside the courtyard; the golden altar, inside the tabernacle.

All those who have been saved by the wonderful grace of God have also received the office of priests. It is their calling to serve in the tabernacle. Their place is at the golden altar, now as true worshipers, to present homage and praise to their God in the power of the Holy Spirit.

"O send out thy light and thy truth: let them lead me; let them bring me unto thy holy hill, and to thy tabernacle. Then will I go unto the altar of God, unto God my exceeding joy" (Psalm 43:3–4). Surely it was the sons of Korah who gave expression to their holy desire with these words. This exultant joy rings out also in their song in Psalm 84. It corresponds exactly to the feelings of all true believers when they sing: "My heart and my flesh cry out unto the living God . . . thine altars, O Jehovah of hosts. . . . Blessed are they that dwell in thy house: they will be still praising thee" (Psalm 84:2–4 ASV).

The sons of Korah knew the altars of God, the brazen altar in the courtyard and also the golden altar of incense in the tabernacle. They sang of the blessedness of those who had the privilege of remaining there for service.

Both the altar of burnt offering and the altar of incense were designated by God as "most holy" (Exodus 29:37; 30:10). Once every year on Yom Kippur, the great Day of Atonement, the four horns of both altars were smeared with the blood of the sin offering of reconciliation. This instruction of God binds the two altars together in our thoughts.

By His shed blood, the Lord Jesus Christ is not only our Savior — as He is termed sixteen times in the New Testament, but now also our High Priest in glory.

The golden altar and *its material* are a type of the Son of God in His special dignity and glory. Here also the acacia

Here the west wall of the tabernacle has been removed to give an open view into the Holy of Holies. The four-colored veil, with the cherubim forms, was fastened to golden clasps and hung on four pillars. The golden walls reflect the curtain.

wood is a picture of His spotless and perfect humanity. He is now, as the Son of man, as the Risen One, in the heavenly glory in His place of honor next to the Father.

Here once more the pure gold covering portrays His deity, as we have already seen. The Lord Jesus Christ is now at the right hand of the Majesty in heaven. Once He suffered judgment in His death on the cross for us, but now the Glorified One stands as *our High Priest* before the presence of God.

The dimensions of the incense altar and the table of shewbread are in remarkable relationship with each other. The table of shewbread was two cubits long and one cubit wide. The golden altar was two cubits high, and one cubit in length and breadth. We want to consider these dimensions briefly.

The table is a type of the Lord Jesus. The Great Shepherd and Overseer of our souls is continually active in service to His redeemed ones. He never loses sight of them. He holds them in His mighty hands; He protects and blesses them in His everlasting care. He is incessantly active on behalf of His own in total dedication of His heart. His own throughout the entire world are secure in His love. The length and breadth of the table speak of this comprehensive care.

The height of the golden altar speaks of Jesus' exclusive activity in heaven, pointing to His holy service that He carries out for us before our God and Father. The Lord Jesus Christ is there for us in the particular dignity of the High Priest.

Jesus is the risen Victor, the great Conqueror. As He triumphantly returned to the Father and neared the

throne of the Highest, He heard the ceremonial oath: "Thou art a priest for ever after the order of Melchizedek" (Psalm 110:4). He did not have that position previously, for that of which Hebrews 9:24 speaks had to take place first: "For Christ is not entered into the holy places made with hands, which are the figures of the true; but into heaven itself, now to appear in the presence of God for us." Since then, the Son serves His God and us in a wonderful dedication, having been chosen by the Father to bear this priestly authority.

On the altar of incense lay a golden plate, which was decorated with a surrounding golden wreath — a picture of the Risen One exercising His priestly ministry as the Crowned One of God.

The high priest is one of the wonderful themes of the Book of Hebrews. Without this divine document we would not know very much about these ministers "of the sanctuary, and of the true tabernacle, which the Lord pitched, and not man" (Hebrews 8:2). The Holy Spirit mentions the great High Priest in the Epistle to the Hebrews ten times, portraying Him in His manifold, blessed activity for His God and His people.

When we consider the instructions God gave to Aaron concerning his ministry at the incense altar, we can clearly understand the meaning of this service. Let us now examine the use of the altar.

The priest "shall take a censer full of burning coals of fire from off the altar before the Lord and his hands full of incense beaten small" (Leviticus 16:12). That was God's ordinance and it was carried out daily, morning and evening, when Aaron trimmed the lamps of the pure candlestick. *This incense* was laid on the burning coals and filled the tabernacle with its sweet-smelling odor.

In Ephesians 5:2 we are reminded of this procedure. The apostle there directs our attention to the fact that the Lord Jesus endured the burning coals of divine judgment and offered Himself to "God as a sweet-smelling sacrifice."

The incense of the altar reminds us of the wonderful love and devotion of the Son to the Father.

"Let my prayer be set forth before thee as incense; and the lifting up of my hands as the evening sacrifice" (Psalm 141:2). In these words, the earnest prayer of the psalmist refers to the ordinances for the offerings.

The priests were instructed to bring the incense two times daily, that is, morning and evening. In contrast, the earnest, sanctified psalmist says emphatically, "But I give myself unto prayer" (Psalm 109:4). But these words also express the intimate relationship between the Lord Jesus and the Father, whose association with each other was always that of the most profound fellowship.

The Holy Spirit's activities are directed toward our becoming — each one of us — like the Lord Jesus. If this is true of us, then our experience of His abundant joy becomes ever deeper and our prayer life will undoubtedly become more richly blessed. Our personal and secret relations with God will no longer be neglected or disturbed by indifference and sin!

The Lord Jesus is the heavenly High Priest and desires to bring *our worship* before God the Father, because He represents us before Him. Only through Christ Jesus is true worship possible and only through Him is it acceptable and precious to God.

These thoughts also lead us to notice the location of the golden altar. It stood directly before the veil, in the area nearest the Holy of Holies — and that is noteworthy. The words of Hebrews 9:1–4 show that the altar of incense was reckoned to the Holy of Holies, as if it stood inside it. This draws our special attention to its significance.

The golden altar is for us a type of the Lord of glory in His most elevated ministry as priest. After His return to heaven, the heart of the Risen One was filled with a special desire, which from that moment on He wished to express in the circle of His disciples: "I will declare thy name unto my brethren: in the midst of the congregation will I praise thee" (Psalm 22:22; cf. Hebrews 2:12).

The Lord Jesus leads the song of praise to His God and stands in holy joy and worshipful homage before Him. What a deeply moving expression of His office as high priest!

He does not desire to bring this worship alone, but rather, "in the midst of the congregation." Honor, thanksgiving, and praise should be brought to the living

God by His redeemed ones, whom the Lord Jesus has made priests to God. There is no greater task on earth! That which will take place in glory and perfection in heaven should already begin here in this world.

It is *in the midst of the church* — among His holy priests — that the Lord Jesus Christ desires to give expression to the longing of His heart. He has promised to be where the redeemed are gathered in His name (Matthew 18:20). It is there that He wishes to be able to reveal Himself and to use His brethren for the priestly ministry of bringing "spiritual sacrifices" (1 Peter 2:5).

In the assembly of the redeemed children of God, no one has a right to assume chairmanship or leadership. Final authority belongs to our High Priest, Jesus Christ, and precludes man's usurpation of authority. In the assembly of the children of God, the willfulness of people will always be found disturbing when it is seen at the table of the Lord, at the Lord's Supper. It infringes on the right of the Lord Jesus and limits the working of the Holy Spirit.

"And upon the first day of the week, when the disciples came together to break bread" — so Luke reports to us about the practice of the disciples of that time (Acts 20:7). It is the privilege of all those who are redeemed by the blood of Jesus to proclaim on the day *of the Lord* the death *of the Lord* at His table. They can take the communion *of the Lord* worthily when it is preceded by an earnest self-judging and the conscience has been made free and the heart filled with joy. Then it is that the Lord can use His saints for priestly ministry. The Lord expects from us a humble attitude, a quiet waiting for, and obedience to, the leading of the Holy Spirit, whose desire is to glorify the Son of God.

Today it is as at the last Passover, as the Lord Jesus said: "With desire I have desired to eat this passover with you before I suffer." Today too it is this desire to be in the midst of His own in the presence of God. Does that move our hearts when we gather at the table of the Lord? Is it the desire of our heart to honor Him in breaking bread in remembrance of Him till He comes? (Luke 22:15; 1 Corinthians 11:23–26).

The Father seeks such as will worship Him in spirit and in truth (John 4:23). The Son wishes, as High Priest, to fulfill this desire of God by eliciting from His church true worship of God the Father. Paul could say of himself and his brethren: "We . . . worship God *in the spirit*" (Philippians 3:3). Are we ready for this service and is our spiritual state such that we are able to perform it?

This is the most exalted service of our High Priest. But in addition, He is active in an indispensable and comforting manner. *As Intercessor,* He remembers all the redeemed and intercedes for them (Romans 8:34). The golden altar reminds us of this.

The four horns on the corners of the covering plate of the altar tell us that this ministry of the Lord Jesus is for the benefit of all saints world-wide; it is a powerful, continual, and effective service of intercession. He meets the manifold needs of the children of God in this world, which is full of danger. In the first place, the Lord Jesus asks for their protection and blessing. All are to reach the glorious goal unharmed. The Lord Jesus, by His intercession, counters all the activity of Satan and the continual temptations that come upon the believer. And in this He is successful, for we read, "He is able also to save them to the uttermost that come unto God by him" (Hebrews 7:25).

Unrepentant sinners have no divine High Priest. This privilege and help is reserved for the redeemed. Our High Priest dedicates His total love to us, and it is the holy desire of the Lord Jesus to keep us completely unharmed amid all the dangers of this world.

Our High Priest has compassion for our weaknesses, but not for our sins. He was here on earth as a man, and as such He subdued the weakness of the body and of the soul in the troubles, temptations, and sufferings of His earthly life. For that reason He is able to help those who are tempted. The Lord expects of us that we "come boldly before the throne of grace, that we may obtain mercy, and find grace to help in time of need" (Hebrews 2:18; 4:14–16).

The two carrying poles on the altar show that the Lord Jesus is active before the Father as both high priest and as comforter.

If the disciples of the Lord fail and become guilty as a result of lukewarmness, self-certainty, and self-will, then the prayer of the Lord insures that the guilty one will be led to repent and confess his sins. It is then that the despondency in his heart yields to faith. Peter actually did experience the love of the Lord through His intercession: "But I have prayed for thee, that thy faith fail not" (Luke 22:32).

But even this does not exhaust the love of the Lord Jesus Christ. He desires to effect the restoration of His disciples — this is the reason for His ministry as manager of our affairs, comforter, and intercessor. "If any man sin, we have an advocate with the Father, Jesus Christ the righteous: and he is the propitiation for our sins" (1 John 2:1–2).

In this, the holy, faithful concern for the total welfare of His own comes to expression. We are totally dependent on the manifold and indispensable ministry of the love of our Lord!

"The altar of incense" was anointed with the holy oil of anointing by Moses and dedicated to God (Exodus 30:25–27). This is underlined and explained in Romans 8:26: "Likewise the Spirit also helpeth our infirmities: for we know not what we should pray for as we ought: but the Spirit itself maketh intercession for us with groanings which cannot be uttered."

God's children have the life of Christ. If this life can unfold in them without being hindered in its effects by unfaithfulness, they will become ever more like Jesus. They will become intercessors like Him and will be able to live in the tabernacle in priestly liberty.

The Holy Spirit has recorded a noteworthy fact concerning the Lord Jesus Christ in Luke's Gospel. Jesus is presented there as the second Adam, the man truly dependent upon God. The evangelist describes how Jesus stood praying in the midst of the multitude after His baptism in the Jordan. It is therefore no wonder that the heavens should open above Him, the Holy Spirit come upon Him, and the voice of the Father point Him out with the words "Thou art my beloved Son; in thee I am well pleased" (Luke 3:21–22). What a wonderful and unique event!

In Luke's Gospel we find Jesus in prayer *ten times.* No wonder that His disciples, deeply influenced by His attitude and His actions, asked Him, "Lord, teach us to pray" (Luke 11:1). Certainly in this we can learn from them.

On the Mount of Transfiguration — the "holy mount" — three of the disciples were with Jesus. It is a thrilling story. "And as he prayed, the fashion of his countenance was altered, and his raiment was white and glistering" (Luke 9:29). Many of us would have our faces changed, even illuminated, if we but prayed as He did.

The warning in the Epistle of Jude should move and motivate us: "But ye, beloved, building up yourselves on your most holy faith, praying in the Holy Ghost, keep yourselves in the love of God" (Jude 20–21). When we pray in the name of Jesus, the High Priest appears with our prayers before the throne of God.

Before He went up to Calvary, the Lord gave to His eleven disciples this important and encouraging promise: "Verily, verily, I say unto you, Whatsoever ye shall ask the Father in my name, he will give it you. Hitherto have ye asked nothing in my name: ask, and ye shall receive, that your joy may be full" (John 16:23–24).

In our prayers we should not use the expression "in His name" as a dead formula. It should be a plea that is in accord with the thoughts, wishes, and interests of the Lord Jesus. God has promised that such prayers will be heard.

It now rests with us to lay claim to this promise and as praying priests to follow the example of our Lord.

5. The Holy of Holies

THE VEIL

Moses and Aaron entered the Holy of Holies from the Holy Place. A veil supported by four pillars separated the two rooms of the dwelling place of God. The front part, the Holy Place, was twenty cubits long and ten cubits wide. The inner part, the Holy of Holies, was cube-shaped; each of its dimensions was ten cubits — in accordance with the instructions of God. The new Jerusalem, "the tabernacle of God with men," likewise has a cubic form: "And the city lieth foursquare, and the length is as large as the breadth" (Revelation 21:16). As we saw at the beginning, the whole structure was so planned by God, for it was to represent "the patterns of things in the heavens" (Hebrews 9:23).

Aaron was permitted to enter the Holy of Holies only once a year. On the great Day of Atonement he passed beyond the curtain into the Holy of Holies, the dwelling place of God, completely clothed in white linen. Except for him, no priest was allowed to enter that most holy place, lest he die.

Also, Aaron was allowed to enter the Holy of Holies only with the blood of the atonement in the offering bowl and surrounded by a cloud of incense that arose from the censer. The heavy veil concealed the ark of the covenant the entire year from the eyes of the servants of God.

The Holy Spirit shows us in Hebrews 10:20 the meaning of this curtain, stating there that it portrays the Redeemer; "The veil, that is to say, his flesh." His earthly appearance — His body — is a miracle of the Holy Spirit, "the mystery of godliness" (1 Timothy 3:16).

The four colors speak very clearly of His glory, as we have already seen. Let us consider them once more in light of Philippians 2:5–11. There we read of Him:

He was "in the form of God," that is, the Son of God. That is the meaning of the blue.

He "took upon him the form of a servant" — as the perfect Servant of the Highest. This corresponds to the scarlet.

He was "found in fashion as a man," as the Son of man. This is portrayed by the white byssus.

He "became obedient unto death, even the death of the cross. Wherefore God also hath highly exalted him, and given him a name which is above every name: that at the name of Jesus every knee should bow . . . and that every tongue should confess that Jesus Christ is Lord," the Lord of Lords, the King of Kings. The purple points to this. All these figures place before us Jesus Christ, the Incomparable One.

The cherubim are particularly noticeable in the embroidery of the veil. What thoughts are associated with it once we have learned the actual meaning of the veil? These mysterious beings are angel princes and naturally turn our thoughts to Genesis 3:24. There we encounter angels for the first time in the Holy Scriptures. These guards were placed to the east before the gate of the

Garden of Eden to prevent the return of the sinful couple into Paradise by means of the flame of the revolving sword. For Adam and Eve there was no return to the happy fellowship with God. The cherubim forms in the veil give testimony to this. The Creator has no relationship with sinful man. Hence, the veil is a definite dividing wall. It is for this reason that it is called the veil.[1]

When God's counsels for the salvation of man were accomplished and God's Son was offered for us, a most remarkable event happened in the temple at Jerusalem. In the hour of our Lord's death, the veil "was rent in twain from the top to the bottom" (Matthew 27:51) "in the midst" (Luke 23:45). The ministering priests — it was the hour for incense, the evening offering — must have witnessed this event in complete astonishment and horror. Rent from top to bottom — that could have been accomplished by no other than the hand of God.

God wanted to show in this unparalleled and decisive hour that the veil had ceased to exist because of the sacrifice of Jesus. The believing sinner now has free access to God. Heaven is open!

It was truly the highest price that could possibly be paid. No one can ever measure what it cost God Himself to make this possible. Two passages in the Holy Scriptures help us to have some idea of what it meant for God to strike the Son of His love with His own hand: "Yet it pleased the Lord to bruise him; he hath put him to grief" (Isaiah 53:10). "Awake, O sword, against my shepherd, and against the man that is my fellow . . . smite the shepherd" (Zechariah 13:7).

[1]In German the veil is called the *Scheidevorhang,* that is, "dividing curtain."

It was possible for the entrance to heaven to be opened only because judgment was executed upon our Savior, Jesus Christ. An unprecedented event! An act of God of immeasurable import! We stand silent and worshipful as we contemplate it.

"The veil . . . was rent in the midst." This detail deserves our attention, for it is of particular significance. The opening could also have been made if the curtain had been torn more to one side. Why, then, down the middle?

How good that the prophetic word from Psalm 102:3,11,23 offers understanding and insight to us on this point. There we hear the man Christ Jesus speaking. The Holy Spirit causes us to think of His person right from the beginning of the psalm: "A prayer of the afflicted, when he is overwhelmed, and poureth out his complaint before the Lord." This lamentation mentions particular details; it speaks of sorrow that His life must prematurely come to a bitter end. This lamentation is repeated in three verses and in verse 24 climaxes in the cry "I said, O my God, take me not away in the midst of my days." With this cry ends His plea for help before the face of God. How old may a believer expect to become, according to Psalm 90:10? "The days of our years are threescore years and ten [seventy]." And the man Jesus died in half this life span. The veil of the temple was rent in two parts down the *middle*. Our hearts are deeply moved by this fact and our gaze is directed toward Him. In so inauspicious a way the Lord Jesus opened heaven and the house of the Father.

The cherubim figures that were woven into the veil have yet more to tell us. It must strike the attention of every observant reader that the angel world is involved in the complete series of events concerned with the work of salvation. The proclamation of the conception of Jesus Christ through the Holy Spirit already came through Gabriel (Luke 1:26–38). Those who proclaimed the good news of the birth of Jesus were an angel of the Lord and a multitude of the heavenly hosts (Luke 2:8–15). Angels were allowed to serve the tempted One, the Conqueror in the desert (Matthew 4:11). The angel who appeared from heaven to strengthen Jesus in Gethsemane performed a most holy service (Luke 22:43). The angelic watch at the open grave of the crucified One was witness to the glorious resurrection of Jesus. The messengers who announced after Jesus' ascension that He would return were likewise angels (Acts 1:10). Angels served Him on many occasions.

The cherubim forms in the veil clearly direct our attention to the fact that the Risen One, Jesus Christ, will come again as the Son of man, "with his mighty angels, in flaming fire," to judge all those who do not obey His gospel (1 Thessalonians 1:7–9).

When the believers of all ages are united before the throne of the Lamb in glory and fall down before Him in worship, then too will the voice of many angels be heard around the throne, myriads of heavenly hosts, saying with a loud voice: "Worthy is the Lamb that was slain to receive power, and riches, and wisdom, and strength, and honour, and glory, and blessing!" (Revelation 5:11–12).

THE FOUR PILLARS OF THE VEIL

The veil was suspended from golden hooks at the upper end of four pillars, which stood at the entrance of the "oracle" (Psalm 28:2). *Oracle* is a term employed sixteen

times in the Old Testament for the Holy of Holies. How meaningful is the number sixteen — two times eight! The ark of God stood in this place — a witness to the glory of the Risen One. The four pillars are a picture of the writers of the four Gospels, to whom was given the task of reporting about the coming of the Son of God, His holy life, His love, His suffering, and His death. In addition, they wrote down His words, which were "full of grace and truth." This was a message of divine love and holy compassion, but also a proclamation of the coming judgment and future glory. "Holy men of God spake as they were moved by the Holy Ghost" (2 Peter 1:21).

The Location of the Pillars

As seen by God, the veil hid these four pillars. This had a special meaning. As we have already seen, a servant always stands behind his lord. For this reason — looking from the inside — the five entrance pillars of the tabernacle are invisible because of the curtain.

In genuine humility and true reverence, the apostles Peter and John were able to bring healing to the lame beggar in the porch called Solomon's "in the name of Jesus Christ," acting as the instruments of God. Peter cried out to the amazed multitude, who attributed this

Four pillars (three pictured) of acacia wood covered with gold stood on bases of silver. They supported the veil, forming the east wall of the Holy of Holies.

deed to *them* and tried to honor them for it: "Why marvel ye at this? or why look ye so earnestly on us, as though by our own power or holiness we had made this man to walk? The God of Abraham . . . hath glorified his Son Jesus" (Acts 3:1–13).

The Material of the Pillars

The four posts of the pillars were made of the same material as the boards of the tabernacle — acacia wood, covered with gold. So we see these pillars also as a picture of those who have received the Lord Jesus Christ as their life into their heart and being and have become partakers of His righteousness and glory. They are pardoned sinners who possess all the riches of salvation.

The bases of the pillars, like those of the boards, are of silver. In this we see the God-given foundation described in 1 Corinthians 3:11: "For other foundation can no man lay than that is laid, which is Jesus Christ."

The Significance of the Pillars

There is, however, a difference between these four pillars and the five pillars of the entrance. Unlike the latter, the four pillars to the entrance of the Holy of Holies had no golden capitals or crowns. Since they may be said to represent the saved person, the question arises: But will they not receive a reward for their service? Certainly each one will receive his reward at the judgment seat of Christ. But where are these signs of honor?

In the immediate area of the ark of the covenant, of the throne of God, no servant will wear his crown. In Revelation 4:8–11, the saints are assembled before the Most High. The four living creatures unceasingly proclaim,

"Behold, the ark of the covenant of the Lord of all the earth"; so the ark is called in the Holy Scriptures (Joshua 3:11). This most holy object was made of acacia wood, completely covered with fine gold, and decorated with a golden wreath.

"Holy, holy, holy, Lord God Almighty." Upon hearing this, the conquerors throw down their crowns saying, "Thou art worthy, O Lord, to receive glory and honour and power." Here is seen only One who is crowned and upon whose head are "many diadems." (Revelation 19:12 ASV). Thus it is that our God, the Father of the Lord Jesus Christ, will fulfill the request of His Beloved: "Glorify thy Son" (John 17:1).

THE ARK OF THE COVENANT

This wonderful ark in the Holy of Holies deserves our careful and close attention. Already the fact that God's Word mentions the ark 180 times stresses its importance. It has different names, which correspond to its worth, purpose, and use: "The ark of the covenant of the Lord of all the earth" (Joshua 3:11), "the ark of the testimony" (Exodus 25:22), "the holy ark" (2 Chronicles 35:3), and also "the ark of thy strength" (Psalm 132:8). The living God connected His holy name with it, and in this way at the same time it represented His holy will, His power, and His glory. *It is the throne of God.*

The Materials of the Ark of the Covenant

The materials that were used are now familiar to us and once again bring before us the glory of the Lord Jesus: The acacia wood — a picture of His wonderful, unique, perfect humanity — and fine gold — a picture of His glorious deity. It is the Lord Jesus who is seen in the ark of the covenant.

The ark of acacia wood was covered inside and out with pure gold. This fact is mentioned twenty-one times. We

already know the symbolical meaning of this number twenty-one (three times seven).

The Dimensions of the Ark

The dimensions of the ark are striking, being entirely different from all the other dimensions of the tabernacle.

The length of this ark or chest was two and a half cubits, the breadth one and a half cubits, and the height likewise one and a half cubits. The thought arises spontaneously as we examine these dimensions that it must be so: He is and remains "chiefest among ten thousand" (Song of Solomon 5:10). In Him is made known the "exceeding riches of his grace" (Ephesians 2:7).

It certainly moves us in a singular way when we see that

the height of the ark of the covenant is exactly the same as the height of the brazen grate of the brazen altar and the height of the table of shewbread. We have already mentioned this correspondence and again wish to return to it.

The burning coals of the altar rested on the grate of brass; the oxygen was drawn in from beneath and produced the hottest fire. This fire is an unmistakable picture of the anger and judgment of God, which consumed the Lamb of God. That means that the One who was offered endured immeasurable suffering and deepest pain.

Afterwards, in symbolism, we find the fruit of the travail of His soul on the golden table, where lay the layers of bread made of the fine flour of the wheat. It is apparent from this that He was "fruitful" (Hosea 13:15) and bore "much fruit" (John 12:24).

> Of Thy soul's anguish shalt Thou enjoy that fruit for which upon the cross Thou didst labor, wrapped in deepest night; perfect, ripe, and holy shall this fruit come before Thee, And Thy divine heart of love will be forever satisfied.

All this — once again in picture — is followed by exceeding glory as reward. Thus we find a most meaningful connection between the brazen altar, the table of shewbread, and the ark of the covenant. The decree of God has made it so.

The Golden Wreath of the Ark of the Covenant

The glory of Jesus Christ was typified by the golden wreath that crowned the ark; this is the third time this decoration is brought to our attention. Everything was made exactly according to the will of our God, who so strongly desired the glorification of the Son. "Thou crownedst him with glory and honour" (Hebrews 2:7).

Full of joy, we look up to Him of whom it is said, "Upon his head were many diadems" (Revelation 19:12 ASV).

At the sight of the golden ark, we experience something similar to the experience of the disciples, who "were eyewitnesses of his majesty" (2 Peter 1:16). The words of Exodus 15:11 thrill us: "Who is like unto thee . . . glorious in holiness . . . ?" We stand before the ark, as it were, in the place where He desires to have His own, "that they may behold my glory" (John 17:24). Already now we behold something of the future glory that will be revealed, and in the Spirit "with open face [behold] as in a glass the glory of the Lord" (2 Corinthians 3:18).

The Rings of Gold

The two carrying staves rested in four rings of gold. The Son of God is the living and wonderful expression of the love of God. The golden rings typify this love.

In the New Testament the Holy Spirit mentions the expression "the love of God" eleven times. This number is characteristic and reminds us of the number of almond blossoms on the golden candlestick and of the number of strips in the goats' hair covering. We have seen that a superabundance is indicated by this number. So also in reference to the love of God, it shows that "the love of God is *shed abroad* in our hearts" (Romans 5:5).

These golden rings are not cited thirty-five times by accident, as already mentioned in the report concerning the tabernacle of God and its components. Thus, seven times five indicates perfect love, by which God binds Himself to the saved children of men — a triumph of divine grace.

Paul desired with his whole heart that all the pardoned children of God might "know the love of Christ, which passeth knowledge" (Ephesians 3:19). It is a great joy for our God when the Holy Spirit can work through this knowledge of Christ's love in you and me, so that our love "may abound more and more" (Philippians 1:9). When this is so, what Paul laid on the hearts of the recently converted Thessalonians will be realized: "And the Lord make you to increase and abound in love one toward another, and toward all men" (1 Thessalonians 3:12).

The Two Carrying Staves

The two carrying staves remind us of two extremely important titles that are given to the Lord Jesus Christ and speak of His work of love: First, He is the one great *Mediator* between God and man, "the man Christ Jesus; who gave himself a ransom for all' (1 Timothy 2:5–6). Only He could have effected our relationship with the living God. No angel would have been able to do so or have been fit for it. It had to be a man, moreover a perfect man, as was our Lord and Savior. This divine Mediator reconciled God and man. What the sin of man had destroyed and what would have remained eternally destroyed without Him was not restored by His intercession, much less by compromises, but by the peace that He made through the blood of His cross (Colossians 1:20).

Moreover, the Lord Jesus is also the holy *Surety* (Hebrews 7:22). His suretyship on our behalf was unspeakably costly. It was His purpose, contrary to His own advice, to sacrifice Himself for the guilt of others: "My son, if thou be surety for thy friend . . . do this now, deliver thyself as a roe" (Proverbs 6:1–5). Despite this, He held firmly to His plan to pay the debt He did not owe. He gave Himself for us and so became the perfect Surety.

That fulfilled so well the words of Psalm 69:4: "I have restored that which I took not away."

The consequences of His loving readiness to intervene were inevitable: He experienced their full bitterness. "He that is surety for a stranger shall smart for it" (Proverbs 11:15). This great shame was literally His lot on the cross: "Take his garment that is surety for a stranger" (Proverbs 20:16; 27:13). "Then the soldiers . . . took his garments . . . and also his coat" (John 19:23).

Through Jesus' deed of love on the cross, we have been given the garments of salvation as a gift: "I will greatly rejoice in the Lord, my soul shall be joyful in my God; for he hath clothed me with the garments of salvation, he hath covered me with the robe of righteousness" (Isaiah 61:10). All who are freed from guilt and shame may rejoice, for they have experienced what is said in Zechariah 3:4: "Behold, I have caused thine iniquity to pass from thee, and I will clothe thee with change of raiment."

The summary of the whole matter contains a wonderful fact: In the Lord Jesus we have — ordained according to the decree of God — the "mediator of the new testament" (Hebrews 9:15) and "a surety of a better testament" (Hebrews 7:22). This testament stands on the unshakable, unique foundation of the grace of God. It is, therefore, no longer endangered by man.

The work of salvation on the cross and the resurrection of Jesus Christ provided the basis for the fulfillment of the unique promise of the new covenant, which was proclaimed through the prophet Jeremiah six hundred years before its fulfillment (Jeremiah 31:31–34).

This new and better covenant does not apply to the church of Jesus Christ, even though all the children of

God today may rejoice in its blessings. The new covenant is addressed exclusively to the house of Israel and the house of Judah, as is made clear by the Holy Spirit in Hebrews 8:6–8, and we rejoice in it.

This is the new covenant that has its sure basis in the blood of the Lamb of God. How gripping are the words of Jesus when He presented the filled cup at the first celebration of His own Supper. He Himself required of His beloved disciples: "Drink ye all of it; for this is my blood of the new testament, which is shed for many for the remission of sins" (Matthew 26:27,28).

The children of God often hear these introductory words at the table of the Lord. Because of them, we rejoice not only in our own salvation, but we also consider that the poured-out blood of our Mediator and Surety benefits other believers; and some day the believing remnant of Israel will pay worshipful homage to Him. Even Israel will be saved only on the basis of this precious blood. Cleansed and redeemed, they will then serve the Lord Jesus, praising Him and glorifying His grace. He will then be their king and Messiah and will lead them into all the promised blessings in His earthly kingdom.

The Holy Spirit speaks of this new covenant a total of nine times — the number that indicates completeness.

THE MERCY SEAT WITH THE CHERUBIM

On top of the ark of the covenant lay a heavy, solid golden covering, called by the Hebrews *kaporeth*. This golden mercy seat is mentioned twenty-seven times in the Old Testament — three times three times three. The trinity of the Godhead is here presented by the number three. Everyone who understands will surely be moved to admiration of the wisdom of God. God ordained the placing of this covering on the golden ark.

The Hebrew verb *kaphar,* from which comes the noun *kapporeth,* means "to cover the sins" or "to reconcile," "to make atonement." A man of God once declared, "I have found a ransom [covering]." It is a wonderful statement and was already given long before Moses (Job 33:24). Later, God made it increasingly clear that He purposed to carry out a plan of love. In His compassion He was ready to lay upon His beloved Son the work of redeeming man. The mercy seat of the ark of the covenant gives witness to this fact.

The dimensions of the mercy seat corresponded exactly to those of the ark.

"To make atonement" — we find this expression seventy-seven times in the Old Testament — seven times eleven. What an overwhelming revelation! The firm purpose of God was to effect salvation for mankind: "But where sin abounded, grace did much more abound" (Romans 5:20).

Two cherubim, one at each end of the covering, stood opposite each other and overshadowed the mercy seat with their wings, their eyes focused on the mercy seat. Covered with beaten gold, they comprised one piece with the covering: "beaten out of one piece" (Exodus 37:7). The cherubim on the veil were interrelated with this. Here they belonged to the ark of God, inseparably connected with the mercy seat.

The impressive forms of the cherubim point to God's omnipotence and righteousness. "Thou hast a mighty arm: strong is thy hand, and high is thy right hand. *Justice and judgment* are the habitation of thy throne" (Psalm

89:13–14). Seven times the Word of God tells us that the Lord sits "between the cherubim" (Psalms 80:1; 99:1). From there Moses once heard the voice of the Almighty: "And there I will meet with thee, and I will commune with thee from above the mercy seat, from between the two cherubim which are upon the ark of the testimony" (Exodus 25:22; cf. Numbers 7:89).

There is a striking difference between "the man of God," as Moses is called in Deuteronomy 33:1, and Aaron, his brother. Moses was allowed to come before the ark with the mercy seat as often as the voice of God called him.

He already had a close association with the living God in his own tent, which he had set up separately, outside the camp. He named this tent "the tent of meeting" (as the tabernacle itself was later named). The cloudy pillar descended upon this tent, and then the eternal God had spoken with Moses face to face, "as a man speaketh unto his friend" (Exodus 33:7–11).

This association between God and Moses remained even after the sanctuary of God was built. There also Moses was allowed to approach the cloudy pillar that

The mercy seat, made of fine gold, was of one piece with the cherubim. The cherubim overshadowed the ark of the covenant with their wings. Their faces were turned toward the mercy seat, where the blood of atonement was sprinkled.

rested on the Holy of Holies. But God did not command His servant Moses to bring blood offerings and incense. The reason for that certainly lies in this, that Moses stands before us in the dignity and authority of the representative of *God*.

Aaron, the high priest, had a completely different position and task. He acted as the representative of a *sinful people* on Yom Kippur, the great Day of Atonement. Therefore he had to be protected by the blood of a bullock and a goat when he entered the Holy of Holies. He entered hidden in a cloud of incense into the presence of God, "that he die not" (Leviticus 16:13–14).

The cherubim were symbols of the power of God in creation and in providence.

How solemn is their significance, as we find in Hebrews 9:5: "And over it the cherubim of glory shadowing the mercy seat." They are the revelation of the holy presence and unapproachableness of God, and at the same time they are the holy royal guard of the majesty of God. Their wings overshadow the ark of the Lord. The angel princes are the protectors of the righteousness of the Most High. "To see thy power and thy glory, as I have seen thee in the sanctuary" (Psalm 63:2).

THE CONTENTS OF THE ARK OF THE COVENANT

Three articles were preserved in the ark: The pot of manna, the rod of Aaron, and the tables of the law. They are of special importance in their symbolism. The ark itself is a picture of our Lord and Savior, and its contents speak likewise of Him whom our souls love.

The ark of the covenant opened to show its contents: the rod of Aaron, which blossomed and bore ripe almonds; the two tables of the law; and the golden pot of manna, the "bread from heaven."

The golden pot of manna. The manna originated in the days in the wilderness, where for forty years God nourished His people He had redeemed out of Egypt. At that time Moses was commanded by God: "Fill an omer of it to be kept for your generations; that they may see the bread wherewith I have fed you in the wilderness" (Exodus 16:32). God called this manna "corn of heaven" or "bread of heaven" (Psalm 78:24; 105:40). The golden pot, which held about two liters (about two quarts), is a picture of our Lord Jesus Christ, who said of Himself: "Moses gave you not that bread from heaven; but my Father giveth you the true bread from heaven. For the bread of God is he which cometh down from heaven, and giveth life unto the world. . . . I am the bread of life: he that cometh to me shall never hunger" (John 6:32–35).

The golden pot of manna was not for the nourishment of the priests; it was to be "preserved" before the Lord God. "He hath made his wonderful works to be remembered: the Lord is gracious and full of compassion. He hath given meat unto them that fear him" (Psalm 111:4–5). Manna is mentioned fifteen times in the Holy Scriptures; three times five represents God's concern for the man who is dependent on Him.

Even today there is a hidden manna. The exalted Lord spoke of it in solemn words when He announced to the assembly of Pergamus: "To him that overcometh will I give to eat of the hidden manna" (Revelation 2:17). Was not the Lord Jesus here thinking and speaking of the "hidden" manna of the ark of the covenant? At any rate, He speaks in this picture of Himself. All believers who, in the name of Christ, swim against the religious tide are overcomers, those who are faithful to Him. They shall be

wonderfully nourished and strengthened by Him. He Himself is their life's bread, the hidden manna, and that is enough. He gives courage to the hearts of the upright. The unseen fellowship with the Son of God is the only basis for a blessed life.

Those who live in this fellowship "shall be satisfied with the goodness of thy house, even of thy holy temple" (Psalm 65:4). This manna strengthens the overcomer and is reserved and promised to them alone. They experience that their "life is hid with Christ in God" (Colossians 3:3).

The Rod of Aaron. This princely rod of almond wood lay one night with the rods of the other eleven princes of Israel before the presence of God in the Holy of Holies. Each rod bore the name of the prince to whom it belonged. The morning following this memorable night, these nobles were amazed when they again took up their rods, for the rod of the tribe of Levi, marked with Aaron's name, blossomed with life. All the others were unchanged — dry and dead as before. By God's power,

Aaron's rod had become a miraculous sign. It was covered with leaves and had produced blossoms. This rod showed life out of death. That it was an almond rod underscores this thought.

We have already seen in commenting on the decoration of the candlestick that the almond tree is the first of all trees in the East to show its white blooms in the spring. It proclaims that the dead plant world is awakened to new life — a picture of the resurrection of the Risen One.

This striking sign was given to the people of Israel immediately following the rebellion of the followers of Korah. These people had intended blasphemously to seize for themselves the office of the priesthood. But by this miraculous sign, God's wisdom made visible and clear who He, in His grace, had selected and marked out to be the high priest (Numbers 16–17). By this means, only Aaron, as a type of the Lord Jesus, was selected, and no one else. This almond staff portrays the Lord Jesus Christ, who is risen from the dead and now possesses an unchangeable priesthood "after the power of an endless life" (Hebrews 7:16–17,25). He is a priest forever so that He may intercede for us. This is a wonderful reality that should fill us with wonder and that, unhappily, we too often do not prize highly enough.

The tables of the law. The prophetic word of Psalm 40 again directs our attention to the Son of God. He gave expression to His purpose in holy joy before God as we see in verse 8: "I delight to do thy will, O my God: yea, thy law is within my heart."

The attitude of the Lord Jesus Christ was always "Thy Word have I hid in mine heart, that I might not sin against thee." His earthly life was marked by the Word: "Thy law is my delight." This expression is found eight times in Psalm 119.

Moses was instructed to put the tables of the law into the ark as a testimony and set it in the Holy of Holies (Exodus 40:20). There they remained "preserved" and intact. At the foot of Sinai, upon seeing the golden calf, Moses — filled with dismay, anger, and indignation — before the eyes of the people smashed the first tables of the law, which had been inscribed by God. This was done as a visible demonstration that Israel had broken the law of God (Exodus 32:19; Deuteronomy 9:8–17).

The Messiah of Israel, "born under the law" (Galatians 4:4 ASV), could in truth testify to His contemporaries: "Think not that I am come to destroy the law, or the prophets: I am not come to destroy, but to fulfill [give the fulness of]" (Matthew 5:17). In the ark of the covenant lay "the testimony," the unbroken tables, a picture of Christ and His perfect obedience.

In the time of Solomon we find only the two tables of the law still in the ark of the covenant. The pot of manna and Aaron's rod had disappeared (1 Kings 8:9). This foreshadows the millennium. At that time the temple of God will be firmly set on Mount Moriah.

God had previously said, "I have gone from tent to tent. . . . Wheresoever I have walked with all Israel"; that is to say, in all places where He commanded that the tent of meeting be erected. This was during the time of the wilderness wanderings (1 Chronicles 17:5), characterized by the signs of divine grace: the manna and the priesthood. Both were indispensable for the continued existence of the people and were of inestimable worth.

In the kingdom of peace of Jesus Christ, however,

righteousness reigns. The tables of the law in the ark are a witness to that (Psalm 66:7; 72:8). Manna and Aaron's rod are no longer necessary.

THE ARK OF THE COVENANT IN THE HOLY OF HOLIES

Being the throne of the Most High in the Most Holy Place, the ark of the covenant is of great significance. This golden ark and its contents, together with the mercy seat and the cherubim, are the focal point of the entire tabernacle.

Although it may seem irrelevant, let me here refer to Proverbs 9:10: "The fear of the Lord is the beginning of wisdom: and the knowledge of the holy is understanding." At first glance this statement hardly bears any relationship to what we have before us; but if we make a careful examination of the words, the verse says, "The fear of the Lord is the beginning of wisdom: and the knowledge of the *Most Holy* is understanding."

Here the expression "the Most Holy" does not indicate the place where the ark of the covenant stood, but rather the person of the Adored One Himself, of whom the ark is a wonderful type.

The Holy Spirit uses such types and likenesses to bring before us ever afresh and to impress deeply upon us the knowledge of the Most High. The "high and lofty one" desires to reveal Himself ever more clearly to our hearts (Isaiah 57:15).

Paul used a striking expression that should fill us with worshipful joy: "For God, who commanded the light to shine out of darkness, hath shined in our hearts, to give the light of the knowledge of the glory of God in the face of Jesus Christ" (2 Corinthians 4:6). This process had been unheard of even for Paul himself, but since his conversion he had only one desire: to know Him. All else he considered loss and refuse in comparison to the exceedingly precious knowledge of the Son of God (Philippians 3:8–10).

The Holy Spirit is active in turning our hearts to our glorified Lord. He desires that we contemplate His love, His perfection, and His worthiness. In this way, the state of our faith and our spiritual growth is richly advanced. "But we all, with open face beholding as in a glass the glory of the Lord, are changed into the same image from glory to glory, even as by the Spirit of the Lord" (2 Corinthians 3:18).

If we look closely at the picture on page 158 showing the ark of the covenant, we see that the cherubim are reflected in the golden walls of the Holy of Holies. This was always true when the "bright cloud," the "excellent glory," filled the dwelling place of God (Matthew 17:5; 2 Peter 1:17). This illustrates the passage from 2 Corinthians quoted above. Whoever dwells in the presence of the glorified Christ will reflect His nature. This is a spiritual law. Only in this way can we be a faithful reflection of Him. Only so can we lead a life pleasing to Him. For this reason the believers in Antioch were first called "Christians" (Acts 11:26). Only in this manner will the world see something in us of the picture of Jesus Christ.

As God is called the "Most Holy," the place where the ark is located also carries the name "the Most Holy Place."

The Most Holy Place is mentioned fourteen times in the Word of God, not without reason: seven times two speaks of perfect witness. In this Most Holy Place God revealed Himself to His people in a special way, and this revelation was to become a communication of enormous importance.

The ark of the Lord stood in the silence of the innermost sanctuary, in the Holy of Holies. The great Day of Atonement was on the tenth day of the seventh month (Leviticus 23:27–28) — the most important celebration for the people of God. Let us therefore consider together closely that which then and there had a special relationship to the ark of the covenant. Let us consider particularly "the image of the things themselves."

On the Day of Atonement the same ceremony was performed year after year. God called the high priest Aaron and entrusted to him a most holy service. He was to cleanse himself with water, lay aside the usual garment of his office, and clothe himself completely in white linen. Then he had to slaughter a number of special sacrificial animals. For himself and for his house he had to bring a young bull as a sin offering and a ram as a burnt offering. He slaughtered the bull first. Above all, the atonement for his own sins had to be performed according to the instructions of God.

First Aaron took a pan full of burning coals, which he had taken from the brazen altar that "stood before Jehovah," where the eternal fire burned (Leviticus 6:5–6). Upon the burning coals he laid two handfuls of the sweet-smelling, pulverized incense, which was quickly burned up. Thus, the high priest was concealed in a fragrant cloud of incense all the while he was in the Holy of Holies. The incense was the first thing that was presented to God (Leviticus 16:12–13).

Let us not forget that Aaron was now in the most holy presence of God. Let the following words be deeply impressed on our innermost being: "That he come not at all times into the holy place within the veil before the mercy seat, which is upon the ark; that he die not: for I will appear in the cloud upon the mercy seat" (Leviticus 16:2).

The cloud of glory, the shekinah, had settled upon the tabernacle after its dedication and filled the Holy of Holies. The high priest now stood before God, the Lord of heaven and earth.

The incense concealed the priest and the mercy seat in a cloud. This is a special picture of the excellency of the Savior, our Lord Jesus.

After this Aaron again approached the ark of the covenant carrying in his hands a golden bowl full of the blood of the sacrifice. He dipped his finger into the blood and sprinkled it upon the front of the mercy seat, between the cherubim, who now looked down upon the redeeming blood. At this moment a miraculous and unique transformation took place.

The ark of the covenant with the mercy seat and the cherubim was the throne of the living God, "the Judge of all the earth" (Genesis 18:25). His unbending righteousness had to demand a terrible judgment for the sinner. The guilty one was threatened by the deserved sentence — the death penalty. This terrible fate could be averted only by one thing — the blood of a pure offering, an innocent creature, which had to die in the place of the sinner. The judgment seat was transformed into a *throne of grace* through this sacrificial blood alone.

The Holy Scriptures give us a clear statement about the throne of grace: "through the redemption that is in Christ

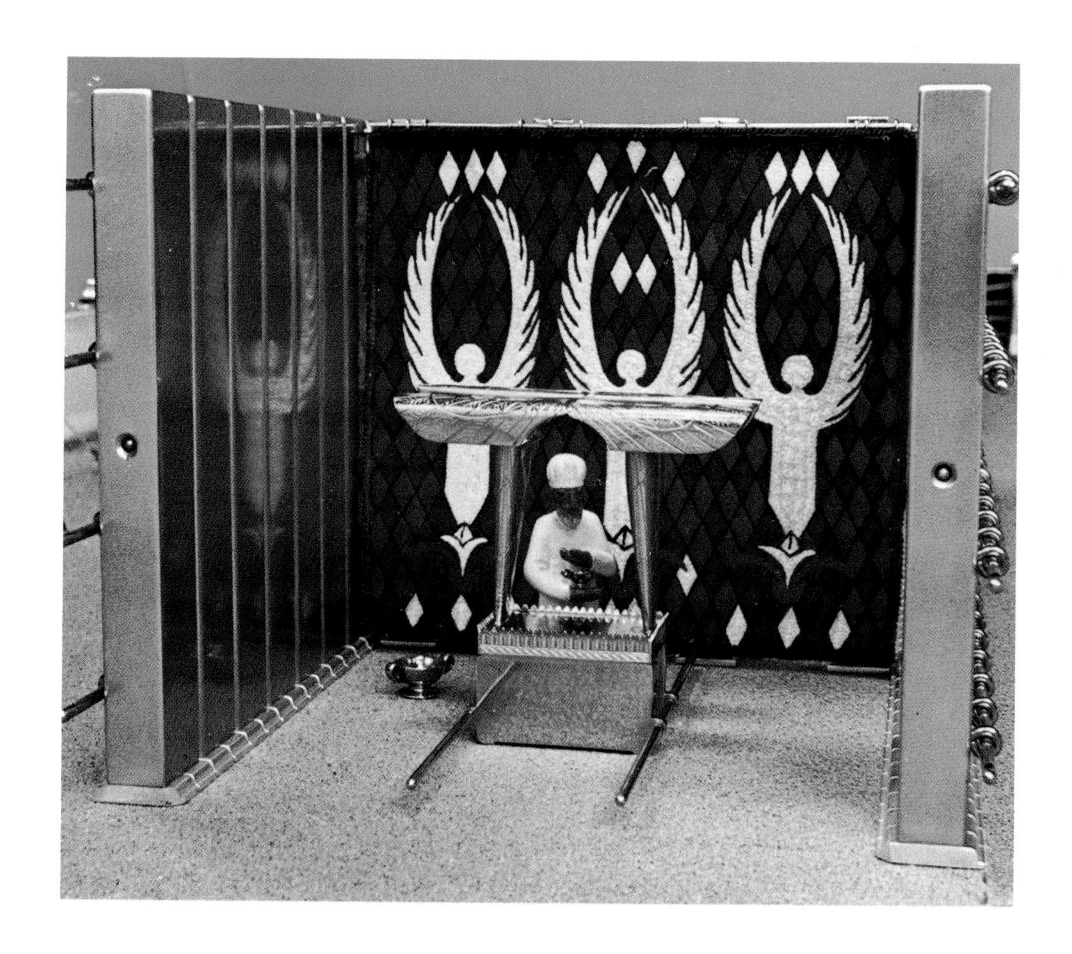

Jesus: whom God hath set forth to be a propitiation [seat of grace] through faith in his blood." This seat of grace is unmistakably the mercy seat of the ark of the covenant. In the Greek, the same word is used for both: *hilasterion* (Romans 3:24–25; Hebrews 9:5). By this, the Holy Spirit shows us that the two terms are equivalent. The ark of the covenant is the seat of grace.

This is the very heart of "the glorious gospel of the blessed God" (1 Timothy 1:11). This fills every believer with adoring wonder and holy joy. Thus, eternal assurance and security is given to all believers — to those who put their complete trust in the blood of the Lamb.

We should particularly notice that Aaron first brought the offering of a young bull for himself and his house. Aaron and his house were by the decree of God separated from the mass of the people. This is of deep significance. We see here the priestly family, whose antitype is the church of Jesus Christ. Of her it is said that she is "an holy priesthood" (1 Peter 2:5). In God's plan of salvation she

The ark of the covenant in the Holy of Holies. The high priest stands before it in a white garment, carrying the bowl of the blood of the sacrifice, which he is sprinkling with his finger seven times on the mercy seat between the cherubim. This occurred every year on Yom Kippur, the great Day of Atonement.

has a special place. The church of Jesus Christ has achieved a wonderful grace and has a unique calling and honor.

By rejecting the Messiah, Israel for a time lost her place of privilege that she had above all peoples. "Through their fall salvation is come unto the Gentiles" (Romans 11:11). It was God's very purpose "to take out of [the Gentiles] a people for his name" (Acts 15:14). All those who have accepted the proffered salvation and have obeyed the call of Jesus Christ belong to this company of the called-out ones: "Vessels of mercy, which he had afore prepared unto glory" (Romans 9:23). They are "partakers of the heavenly calling" (Hebrews 3:1).

It was God's plan that we should be brought into fellowship with Him, for He wants to have us in His most intimate presence. That was made possible only through the offering on Calvary. The young bull that was offered for Aaron and his house is the prophetic picture of the Offering of Calvary. In this way was fulfilled that of which the prophet called out: "Peace, peace to him that is far off, and to him that is near" (Isaiah 57:19). Those who are "far off" were to be the first to partake of this peace! And we who are of the nations belong to it. "But now in Christ Jesus ye who sometimes were far off are made nigh by the blood of Christ" (Ephesians 2:13). "And he came and preached peace to you that were far off and peace to them that were nigh" (Ephesians 2:17 ASV).

For this reason we should say with one voice and out of an overflowing heart in praise to our God: "Unto him be glory in the church by Christ Jesus throughout all ages, world without end" (Ephesians 3:21).

God's love is wonderfully revealed and glorified

through the work of our Lord Jesus Christ. Through the costly blood of Jesus Christ, God's eternal councils of grace are fulfilled: "Righteousness and peace have kissed each other" (Psalm 85:10).

Let us remember once again that only Aaron and his house could step into the immediate presence of God. The people of Israel were not able at that time to experience this wonderful access, this intimate nearness and close fellowship with God. This is now all revealed and given to the church of the living God. It is clearly shown to her in the Word of God that this wonderful calling — to make the heart of God glad and to reciprocate His love — is already hers here on earth.

"Having therefore, brethren, boldness to enter into the holiest by the blood of Jesus . . . let us draw near with a true heart in full assurance of faith, having our hearts sprinkled from an evil conscience, and our bodies washed with pure water" (Hebrews 10:19–22).

This relationship with the living God and the privilege of living before the face of the Highest remains for all eternity the foremost task of the church of Jesus Christ, the bride of the Lamb.

A second sacrifice followed the personal cleansing of Aaron. Aaron now had to slaughter the ram of the sin offering for the people. With the blood of this sacrifice, the following took place: "Then shall he . . . do with that blood as he did with the blood of the bullock, and sprinkle it upon the mercy seat, and before the mercy seat" (Leviticus 16:15).

This scene is full of meaning. It foreshadows the fact that atonement and reconciliation for the believing remnant of the people of Israel are based on the blood of Jesus.

There is a deep significance in the fact that it is mentioned only in the second place in Leviticus 16. Thus, what Paul tells us in Romans is fulfilled: "Until the fullness of the Gentiles be come in, and so all Israel shall be saved" (Romans 11:25–26).

After Aaron had sprinkled the sacrificial blood on the mercy seat, he again dipped his finger into the golden bowl and sprinkled the blood "seven times before the mercy seat." At the very feet of Aaron the ground was moistened with the atoning blood. The high priest stood on blood-sprinkled soil. That is a gripping picture that points to a more inclusive effect of this holy ministry. Here we are shown in the clearest possible way that the saving power of the blood of Jesus Christ is not for the benefit of man only. It affects the whole of creation: The blood was sprinkled *upon the earth* (Leviticus 16:14).

When John the Baptist saw the Lord Jesus on the bank of the Jordan, he uttered the prophetic words: "Behold the Lamb of God, which taketh away the sin of the world" (John 1:29). The expression "the sin of the world" does not mean the guilt of all sinners, but rather the curse of sin that came on the whole of creation through the transgression of Adam. So the Word declares: "The creature itself also shall be delivered from the bondage of corruption [transitoriness] into the glorious liberty of the children of God" (Romans 8:21).

Here we see what the blood of the Lamb has done and how exceedingly far His reconciling power reaches.

Seven times Aaron sprinkled the blood on the ground. This points to the fact that in the millenium the entire creation will be wonderfully and perfectly delivered from the curse of sin. "The wilderness and the solitary place shall be glad for them; and the desert shall rejoice, and blossom as the rose. It shall blossom abundantly, and rejoice even with joy and singing: the glory of Lebanon shall be given unto it, the excellency of Carmel and Sharon, they shall see the glory of the Lord, and the excellency of our God" (Isaiah 35:1–2).

If we reflect on these processes, we can but remember the words that show us the worth and the meaning of the blood of Jesus Christ in its proper light. When we comprehend with our hearts the full extent of this, we will be filled with an unchanging peace.

"But Christ being come an high priest of good things to come, by a greater and more perfect tabernacle, not made with hands, that is to say, not of this building; neither by the blood of goats and calves, but by his own blood he entered in once into the holy place, having obtained eternal redemption for us" (Hebrews 9:11–12).

THE HOLY GARMENTS OF THE HIGH PRIEST

Seven special articles of clothing and ornaments composed the official apparel of the high priest: the robe, the embroidered coat, the ephod, the belt of the ephod, the breastplate, the mitre, and the diadem.

They were all prescribed for the high priest "for glory and beauty" (Exodus 28:2,40). God calls to His people, who know how to regard the significance of the anointed priest: "Wherefore, holy brethren, partakers of the heavenly calling, consider the Apostle and High Priest of our profession, Christ Jesus. . . . For this man was counted worthy" (Hebrews 3:1,3).

The Lord Jesus could not exercise the dignity of the

office of a high priest during His earthly life, because He was the son of David, of the tribe of Judah. Only the sons of Aaron, of the tribe of Levi, were set apart for this ministry (Hebrews 7:13,14; 8:4).

The Father first conferred on the Son by a special oath, after His resurrection and ascension, the eternal priesthood after the order of Melchisedek (Hebrews 7:14–21). The Lord Jesus Christ did not usurp this honor, but rather the Father, who said to him, "Thou art my Son," conferred it on Him (Hebrews 5:5).

Aaron's ministry was carried out in all weakness in the tabernacle that stood in the wilderness of Sinai. The Lord Jesus Christ exercises His ministry as high priest in the glory of heaven in the true sanctuary, and this ministry is unchangeable and eternal (Hebrews 6:20; 7:28). This ministry of the Lord Jesus is of immeasurable importance for the pardoned and elect children of God. Ten times the Epistle to the Hebrews speaks to believers concerning their High Priest, who now appears before the face of God to represent them (Hebrews 9:24). He is there by virtue of His blood that was shed on the cross. The blood of Jesus alone is the wonderful and blessed foundation of our relationship with the God of glory.

Understanding and compassion, mercy and comfort, help and a listening ear, grace and power — we may experience all of these through Jesus, our High Priest. As our "forerunner," He has already reached the goal, and we have the firm assurance that He will bring us there too. During the time of our earthly existence in a world full of sin, misery, and corruption, He intercedes for us. "Wherefore he is able also to save them to the uttermost that come unto God by him" (Hebrews 7:25).

The high priest in his holy garments "for glory and beauty." Over the white robe he wore a blue coat. His chest and back were covered with the four-colored, gold-embroidered ephod.

We are not left alone. He is our Surety that we will be led safely through all misery and need.

In Hebrews we read of the important difference between Aaron and the Lord Jesus: "And every priest *standeth* daily ministering. . . . But this man . . . forever *sat down* on the right hand of God" (Hebrews 10:11–12).

"Now of the things which we have spoken this is the sum: We have such an high priest, who is set on the right hand of the throne of the Majesty in the heavens; a minister of the sanctuary, and of the true tabernacle, which the Lord pitched, and not man" (Hebrews 8:1–2).

We must not lose heart in the tribulations of this present time. The Word gives us new courage and new power: "Let us run with patience the race that is set before us, looking unto Jesus the author and finisher of our faith" (Hebrews 12:1–2).

Indeed, how much we owe to the Lord Jesus: thanksgiving, worship, praise, and honor.

The details of the high priest's garments speak of the Lord Jesus in His glory. They help us the better to recognize His incomparable qualities and the worth of His person, in order that we will love and honor our Lord more.

The Robe

The robe of the high priest with its belt of bysus was made of finely woven fabric. The spotless white of the cotton was of the finest possible quality, and could not be imitated.

This also illustrates for us the personal perfection and purity of the man Christ Jesus. He is the "Just One." He is given this title of honor seven times in the New Testament.

Our High Priest is enthroned above with the Father as a perfect Man — a fact of immeasurable significance. We are represented before God by a glorified *Man,* and in Him God is wholly pleased.

"For such an high priest became us, who is holy, harmless, undefiled, separate from sinners, and made higher than the heavens" (Hebrews 7:26), who "was in all points tempted like as we are, yet without sin" (Hebrews 4:15). Therefore His intercession and petition for us before the majesty of God is of the highest importance.

The Coat

The coat of the high priest was entirely of blue. This is again a reference to the heavenly origin, the character, and the ministry of our Lord and Savior. He came from heaven and has gone to heaven. There He represents His heavenly people whom He will lead to glory to the place determined by God.

The bells of pure gold portray His testimony. They were fastened to the bottom of the garment alternately with pomegranates. The ringing of these golden bells is a sound from the heavenly tabernacle. The pure gold, out of which the bells were made, testifies of Christ's deity and witnesses of His love.

On the day of Pentecost, ten days after the ascension of the Risen One, the people of Jerusalem had an unusual experience. A message from heaven was heard, answering to the sound of the golden bells. The Holy Spirit witnessed of the glorified Christ. Three thousand people were moved in their hearts by this sound and accepted salvation in Jesus Christ.

Pomegranates, with their pronounced richness in seeds, are a splendid picture of the incomparable fruitfulness and vigor of life. The Lord Jesus Christ is powerful and fruitful in His ministry for us; He is ministering for us in complete glory, as is illustrated by the three colors: The pomegranates were arranged alternately in colors of blue, purple, and scarlet.

Wonderful, varied fruits were produced by the first Christians at Pentecost. One could see in them the fullness of the life of the Lord Jesus Christ. They were filled with His love. To the amazement of those around them, their actions were completely changed. Heavenly life and royal bearing, but also a readiness to suffer, were apparent in them. A happy life of fellowship came into being and continued among them. These were "fruits of righteousness, which are by Jesus Christ, unto the glory and praise of God" (Philippians 1:11).

The Ephod

The ephod consisted of two shoulder pieces that were fastened together and reached nearly to the knee. They covered the back and the chest. The yarn of which it was made was bright with the colors blue, purple, and scarlet; also white byssus was present. This embroidered cloth was woven with threads of beaten gold. It was a marvelous piece of work, full of beauty and glory. The whole was a type of the nature of the Son of God in His high-priestly honor — a picture of divine glory. God bestowed this honor on Him only because the Lord Jesus bore the judgment on the cross and because He arose afterward. "So also Christ glorified not himself to be made an high priest; but he that said unto him, Thou art my Son, today have I begotten thee. As he saith also in another place, Thou art a priest forever after the order of Melchisedec" (Hebrews 5:5–6).

Concerning Aaron, the high priest, God said, I chose "him out of all the tribes of Israel to be my priest, to offer upon mine altar, to burn incense, to wear an ephod before me" (1 Samuel 2:28).

Today the people of Israel are characterized by a prophecy of the utmost importance: "The children of Israel shall abide many days without a king, and without a prince, and without a sacrifice . . . and without an ephod." They have no high priest who could enter in the beauty of the ephod before God for them. They are a people "without an ephod," because they rejected the true, heavenly Sent One of God. The tragic consequences of this decision are clearly placed before us. In consequence, Israel must still go through terrible judgments.

In spite of this, God sent a comforting promise to His earthly people through Hosea: "Afterward shall the children of Israel return, and seek the Lord their God, and David their king; and shall fear the Lord and his goodness in the latter days" (Hosea 3:4–5).

But the heavenly people of God, the pardoned and redeemed of the Lord Jesus, rejoice in their High Priest, who is at the right hand of the Majesty on high and who represents them day and night.

The fasteners of the shoulder pieces of the ephod were remarkable, for there two large gems set in gold bore the names of six of the tribes of Israel, each precious stone having six names engraved on it, like the engraving of a signet. In a related sense, they tell us that the blood-bought church is unforgettable for God. In this, each believer may see a sign that the Father in heaven continually remembers His children. "Yet will I not forget thee" (Isaiah 49:15). That is indeed a promise full of comfort, vividly pictured by the names on the onyx — the "stones of memorial" (Exodus 28:12). "Thou shalt not be forgotten of me" (Isaiah 44:21).

The Belt of the Ephod

He who has girded himself shows that he stands ready for service. This splendid girdle testifies of the high-priestly ministry. It is called "the curious girdle" and was made of the same material as the ephod robe. Executed in embroidery work, it characterizes the unique, perfect ministry of our Lord.

When He washed the disciples' feet, the Lord Jesus wore the linen girdle — a picture of perfect humility. He took upon Himself at that moment the form of a servant to enable His own to have fellowship with Him (John 13).

Today in glory the Lord Jesus wears the magnificent girdle of the ephod. As our High Priest, He brings to the Father the "supplications, prayers, intercessions, and giving of thanks" of His people (1 Timothy 2:1).

The Breastplate

On the ephod, above the girdle, the high priest wore an article that consisted of the same fabric as the other two parts of the priestly garment. Also here, gold, blue, purple, scarlet, and byssus were visibly woven together. Each side of the square breastplate measured a handbreadth. The two pieces of cloth of equal size were bound together at the bottom; open above, they formed a container, a kind of pocket. In them were laid the "Urim and Thummim." On the front side, the breastplate was decorated with twelve precious stones. Each of these sparkling stones was distinct. Each shone in a different color when the light of the golden candlestick fell upon it. A more detailed description of these jewels is given in the section on the heave offering.

The breastplate received its name from the fact that it was worn on the breast of the high priest. God's Word required that it be carefully fastened to the garment of the ephod. Chains of braided gold and golden rings with loops of blue secured the breastplate in position. It was to rest on the heart of the anointed priest without being displaced.

"And Aaron shall bear the names of the children of

Israel in the breastplate of judgment upon his heart, when he goeth in unto the holy place, for a memorial before the Lord continually. And thou shalt put in the breastplate of judgment the Urim and the Thummim [lights and perfections], and they shall be upon Aaron's heart . . . continually" (Exodus 28:29–30). The expression "the breastplate of judgment" means "administration of justice" or "pronouncement of judgment."

The high priest carried the names of the twelve tribes of Israel on his shoulders and on his heart. When decisions were to be asked of God, the Urim and Thummim gave expression to the wisdom of God. How meaningful these pictures are! Jesus Christ the High Priest carries His blood-bought saints upon His loving heart and with the strength of His shoulders. They are entrusted to His unceasing care.

The names of the redeemed are indelibly engraved in precious stones as a memorial before God. This wonderfully reveals the worth and importance of the precious stones and their God-ordained distinction as a picture of the children of God.

These gleaming stones, set in gold on the breastplate, were "for beauty and glory." Thus may every believer be joyfully aware that he is a part of the glory and adornment of His Lord and Savior.

In His high-priestly prayer, the Lord Jesus testified concerning all who were given to Him by the Father: "For them which thou hast given me. . . . I am glorified in them" (John 17:9–10). Paul also wrote about his beloved brethren and fellow workers: "They are . . . the glory of Christ" (2 Corinthians 8:23).

Let us praise our Lord and Savior in worship and homage, He who in His incomprehensible grace has given His own such an exalted place.

Three times is the breastplate called the "breastplate of judgment." This is to make clear that the Lord will in perfect wisdom and righteousness provide redress for His oppressed ones. To all who truly trust Him, he says, "And shall not God avenge his own elect, which cry day and night unto him, though he bear long with them? I tell you that he will avenge them speedily" (Luke 18:7–8). Even though the promise is primarily addressed to the believing remnant of Israel, it will still be fulfilled for all witnesses of the faith. The triple mention of the breastplate assured divine justice and vindication for the oppressed saints in due time. We can surely apply this also to the judgment seat of Christ (2 Corinthians 5:10).

At the same time we know from Holy Scriptures that God has promised His own that He will preserve them in holy faithfulness during their earthly existence. "He loveth righteousness and judgment" (Psalm 33:5). "The Lord executeth righteousness and judgment" (Psalm 103:6). "He leadeth me in the paths of righteousness for his name's sake" (Psalm 23:3).

Eighteen times, the Word of God speaks of the breastplate (two times nine is eighteen). The number two means "witness"; nine has the sense of "completion."

It is the expression of the divine will to reveal the fullness of His grace in perfection, when the counsels of His wisdom and love are fulfilled. "That in the ages to come he might shew the exceeding riches of his grace in his kindness toward us through Christ Jesus . . . to the praise of his glory" (Ephesians 1:14; 2:7).

The Holy Diadem on the Headdress

As the crowning feature of the entire holy vesture, the high priest wore a diadem of fine gold on a white headdress of byssus. Of this, the Word of God says, "And they made the plate of the holy crown of pure gold, and wrote upon it a writing, like to the engravings of a signet, HOLINESS TO THE LORD. And they tied unto it a lace of blue, to fasten it on high upon the mitre; as the Lord commanded Moses" (Exodus 39:30–31).

What was the function of this splendid decoration? "And it shall be upon Aaron's forehead, that Aaron may bear the iniquity of the holy things, which the children of Israel shall hallow in all their holy gifts; and it shall be always upon his forehead, *that they may be accepted before the Lord*" (Exodus 28:38).

The people of God had the glorious calling, as a priestly race, to serve in the presence of God; they were to bring Him thanksgiving, praise, and worship as an offering. He seeks such as His worshipers (John 4:23). His worshipers are able to fulfill this desire of God in humility and holy reverence, in spirit and in truth. They perform this ministry as "an holy priesthood, to offer up spiritual sacrifices, acceptable to God by Jesus Christ" (1 Peter 2:5).

In the sacrificial services of Israel, the holy diadem was the visible expression of acceptability before God. Naturally, a variety of imperfections, weaknesses, or failures could creep into this ministry. It was, therefore, always important to every upright Israelite that the high priest — graced with the holy diadem — exercise all priestly duties in a manner appropriate to the holiness of God. Only in this way could they meet His approval.

The true worshiper sees a comforting, encouraging picture of the grace of God in the diadem. Only grace makes it possible to exercise spiritual service in freedom of spirit. "Having therefore, brethren, boldness to enter into the holiest by the blood of Jesus . . . having an high priest over the house of God; let us draw near with a true heart in full assurance of faith" (Hebrews 10:19,21–22).

We enter God's holy presence because He has called us, sanctified us, and made us worthy to do so, and because our great High Priest presents our offerings on our behalf. For Jesus' sake, the pleasure of God rests on us.

"Then will I go unto the altar of God, unto God my exceeding joy: yea, upon the harp will I praise thee, O God my God" (Psalm 43:4).

"Accepted in the beloved" (Ephesians 1:6) — before the presence of the living God!

We have been led into the tabernacle to view the glory of the Lord. How good it is when the Holy Spirit is our Guide, and we have fulfilled His desire.

THE COMPLETED WORK

"So Moses finished the work. Then a cloud covered the tent of the congregation, and the glory of the Lord filled the tabernacle. And Moses was not able to enter into the tent of the congregation, because the cloud abode thereon, and the glory of the Lord filled the tabernacle" (Exodus 40:33–35).

"And on the day that the tabernacle was reared up the cloud covered the tabernacle, namely, the tent of the testimony: and at even there was upon the tabernacle as it were the appearance of fire, until the morning" (Numbers 9:15).

"The cloud of glory" — the visible sign of the presence of God — was not unknown to Israel. During the exodus from Egypt, the people received guidance and light from the pillar of cloud and the pillar of fire. The pillars protected the assembly of the Lord and gave them victory over the foe (Exodus 13:21; 14:19–20). But now this shekinah stayed among them, a visible sign of the presence of God so rich in grace. It was a testimony of His glory and holiness (Numbers 14:14).

God speaks of this cloud fifty-six times in the Old Testament. The cloud is the uniting focal point for the people of the Lord. Where the cloud stood was the center of a united people. They were blessed and led, illuminated and preserved by God. God, in His wonderful condescension and love, desired to have fellowship with His people. "For thou art an holy people unto the Lord thy God: the Lord thy God hath chosen thee to be a special people unto himself, above all people that are upon the face of the earth. The Lord did not set his love upon you, nor choose you, because ye were more in number than any people; for ye were the fewest of all people: But because the Lord loved you" (Deuteronomy 7:6–8).

The tent of meeting inside the courtyard. The smoke of the sacrificial fire rose and the cloud of the glory of God descended and filled the dwelling. In this way, the presence of the Highest was visibly revealed to His people.

How much more do these words apply to all those who are redeemed, cleansed, and sanctified, "called . . . out of darkness into his marvelous light" (1 Peter 2:9). This has become true of them: "And it shall come to pass, that in the place where it was said unto them, Ye are not my people; there shall they be called the children of the living God" (Romans 9:26).

They are all called to gather themselves around Him who has promised His holy presence where two or three are gathered together in His name (Matthew 18:20).

Figuratively speaking, the cloud of glory is still present today. Are we at home there? Is it our heart's desire to be where the Lord of glory awaits us?

God has richly blessed us. The "example and shadow of heavenly things" move our innermost being. Their purpose is to place before our eyes and heart a fullness of the glories of our Lord Jesus Christ.

Then, full of holy wonder, we may worshipfully join in the words of the Holy Spirit: "For who hath known the mind of the Lord? or who hath been his counsellor? . . . For of him, and through him, and to him, are all things: to whom be glory for ever. Amen" (Romans 11:34,36).

"Unto him be glory in the church by Christ Jesus throughout all ages, world without end. Amen" (Ephesians 3:21).

Give grace, Father, that the wonderful fullness
of Thy Word may be unveiled to our sight
and we may see the great depths of wisdom,
so that, secured by Thy eternal truth,
we may walk in the clear light of the Word
on the path of faithfulness, renewed and unstumbling.

BIBLIOGRAPHY

Dennett, E. *Typical Teachings of Exodus.* 6th ed. London: A. S. Rouse, 1906.

Mackintosh, C. H. *Notes on the Pentateuch.* Exodus, vol. 2; Leviticus, vol. 3; Deuteronomy, vols. 5 and 6. Old Tappan, N. J.: Revell, n.d.

Pollock, A. J. *The Tabernacle's Typical Teachings.* London: Pickering and Inglis, n.d.

Rhind, W. G. *The High Priest of Israel.* London: Samuel Bagster and Sons, 1868.

———. *The Tabernacle in the Wilderness.* 5th ed. London: W. H. Broom, 1860.

Ridout, S. *Lectures on the Tabernacle.* Neptune, N. J.: Loizeaux, 1952.

Soltau, H. W. *The Holy Vessels and Furniture of the Tabernacle.* Grand Rapids: Kregel, 1969.

———. *The Tabernacle, the Priesthood and the Offerings.* Grand Rapids, Kregel, n.d.